B.
MUKAI,

LIVING WITH DYING

LIVING WITH DYING
A Personal Journey

Linda Pratt Mukai
Janis Fisher Chan

Butterfield Press
San Anselmo, California

Developmental Editor: Judy Hulka
Copyeditor: Lynn Ferar
Production Management: Melanie Field, Strawberry Field Publishing
Composition: Christi Payne, Book Arts
Interior and Cover Design: Suzanne Montazer, SLM Graphics
Printer: Bookcrafters, Chelsea, Michigan

Butterfield Press
P.O. Box 2522
San Anselmo, CA 94979-2522
phone: 415-456-1781
fax: 415-456-9506

Library of Congress Cataloging-in-Publication Data
Mukai, Linda Pratt
     Living with dying : a personal journey / by Linda Pratt Mukai
     and Janis Fisher Chan.
          p.   cm.
     Includes bibliographical references.
     ISBN 0-9650961-0-6
     1. Mukai, Linda Pratt—Health.   2. Colon (Anatomy)—
Cancer—Patients—California—Biography.   I. Chan, Janis Fisher.
II. Title.
RC280.C6M83   1996
362.1'96994347—dc20
[B]   96-15212
                                                                    CIP

p. 89 *Sacred Clowns* by Tony Hillerman. Copyright © 1993 by Tony
Hillerman. Reprinted by permission of HarperCollins Publishers Inc.

Introduction

⤜⤛

Three weeks after I was diagnosed with metastatic colon cancer in June 1992, I asked Janis Chan to help me write this book. By then we had known each other for almost ten years. I had been her client when I was head of the training and development department for Shaklee Corporation in San Francisco, and we worked together on several more projects after I started my own management consulting business. Over the years, I came to know her not only as an exquisitely trained writer, but also as an excellent collaborator—creative, intuitive, hard-driving, and fun to work with.

I think I originally asked Janis to work with me on this book so she would goad me into giving it time each week, discipline me to get it done, and be a sounding board and an advisor on the direction to take. She has done these things and much, much more. She has overlaid her feelings and her perspective, and she has pushed my thinking into new spheres by asking tough, probing, analytical questions. She has become an even closer friend, riding all the waves of hope and despair with me. Now she has to finish the book for me because my abilities are declining.

When we began, we weren't certain what the book would be about. I had scoured the bookstores, looking for something that would tell me, an average noncelebrity, how to cope with cancer and all it brings. Within a week of my diagnosis, I recognized that having cancer was more than a physical problem. It was a huge

1

communications challenge. It was changing the way I related to others. I had to find ways to tell people I had cancer. I had to cope with their reactions and, sometimes, their lack of response since they didn't know what to say. I had to ask doctors the right questions during the few minutes they allowed for answering questions. I had to ask people for help when *I* had always been the caretaker. I also had to cope with enormous life-changing events and issues, such as bringing to a close the career I had craved and nurtured, giving up my privacy when I couldn't do things for myself, losing and gaining friends as people sorted themselves out based on how much they could handle, resolving or letting go of differences with family members, and confronting the cold reality of my pending death and its effects on everyone around me.

I've been told that I'm compulsive and obsessive about doing things right, that I'm too much of a perfectionist. My pastor, Dave Steele, once accused me of trying to "die right." I accept all such criticism as accurate and true. But I am now living my last days, and I want each one to be special. I want to remain as able as I can to ask for what I want and need. I have told my husband, Craig, that I want him to be with me in my final days and minutes. I want to make more memories for Craig and my nine-year-old son, Matt. I want to continue to learn and to grow as a person during this last experience. I know it will be the most difficult journey I will ever take, and I want to take it with as much courage and dignity as I can. I want to be ready when death comes, and until then I want to live every moment.

Although each person's experience with cancer is very different, we all have relationships and communicate with others every day. I am sharing my story and the choices I made so that other patients who are living with terminal cancer, and their friends, families, and caregivers, may be better prepared to choose what's right for them.

Linda Mukai
July 30, 1994

Prologue

On July 3, 1992, my friend and colleague Linda Mukai called to tell me she had colon cancer. She sounded healthy and strong on the telephone: "I'm going to put you on the speaker phone so I can eat my toast. Isn't that rude?" Then she said, "There's no nice way to say it. I've got cancer."

I said, "Oh, my God. Oh, Linda, I'm so sorry." I rambled on, not knowing what to say. Always a good listener, she let me go on for a while. Finally I said, "Is there anything I can do?"

"Yes," she said. "You can help me write a book."

Of course I said yes. I knew exactly why she wanted to do it. It's what people like us do to stay in control—turn a crisis into a project. We know how to get through a series of tasks. Getting through life is much harder.

"Do you have the time?" Linda asked.

"I'll make the time," I said.

I said I'd help, but I was frightened. Somehow, I'd managed to avoid directly confronting death, even though I was already in my early fifties. At the time, no one close to me had died, except my grandparents. Would I really be able to sit with Linda week after week recording her journey towards the end of her life?

But Linda was giving me a gift—a very special gift, as I was to learn. So I said yes. At the same time, I wondered what in the world I was getting myself into.

We met a few days later in Linda's bedroom with its king-sized waterbed and a giant grey stuffed elephant by the door that opens into a spacious back yard. Linda laughed as she talked about waiting in lines with her friend Sue Darling at the bank and the hospital, about their idea for a T-shirt slogan: "I'm a cancer patient, fast service please!" She seemed strangely delighted with her new insider's take on the world. I knew the laughter was necessary. But I could not laugh. I thought, "This is *not* a laughing matter."

"Should we write some objectives?" Linda asked. As consultants, that's how we always start our projects. But this was different. "Let's just feel our way through," I said, and she agreed.

And that's what we've done, felt our way. For me it's been like walking on tiptoe in the dark—tentative, afraid of stepping on something sharp or gushy. I remain curiously detached most of the time, although sometimes tears come unexpectedly, especially when Linda talks about her husband Craig and her son Matt, when I sense her sadness at the prospect of leaving the people she loves.

When we began our work, Linda was reading Gilda Radner's book, *It's Always Something*. I knew I should read it, too, but I didn't want to. My husband worried that I would bring it all home, that Linda's book would become one of my obsessions. I worried that I would not be able to talk to him about it because it might bring back the pain of his mother's death—she was almost the same age as Linda when she died.

We met every week at first, less often as time passed, except when there was a crisis, and then more often when Linda's condition worsened. I tried to listen carefully and ask good questions. I learned to notice when I started to refer to Linda's cancer as "it," when I began thinking more about the thing than the person. I learned to recognize my own fear, and the embarrassment that followed, and to remind myself, "This is not happening to me."

When we began, I already admired and respected Linda for her wit, her creativity, her intelligence, her assertiveness, and her ability to get things done while remaining calm (on the outside, at least) and compassionate. As we've worked on this book, I've come to know her far better than I would have otherwise—we were both so busy, so focussed on our businesses, projects, and the myriad tasks that always need doing. Without this book, we might never have found the time to nurture our friendship.

Now, we're not only friends, my admiration for Linda has increased a thousandfold. Throughout her ordeal she has been incredibly strong, incredibly clear and thoughtful. In her own unique way, she has transformed her experience with a terminal disease into an opportunity—a time of learning and a time of growth. Everyone fortunate enough to be close to her during this time shares in this opportunity, and we will not come away unchanged.

Janis Fisher Chan
August 3, 1994

DIAGNOSIS

Getting the News

When we first discovered I had cancer, Craig and I
hugged each other and started crying. I said, "Craig,
I always thought I was going to die from a heart attack!"
And he said, "Well, don't worry, maybe you still will."

In February 1992, I began getting abdominal pains that felt like severe constipation. Having been constipated all my life, I ignored them. I was busy. I had two huge projects, one for Levi Strauss and one for IBM. I didn't have time to be bothered with physical problems, even though sometimes the pain was overwhelming. I thought, "Just increase the lettuce, you're not eating well, do the fibers and berries thing some more. Take Maalox and hang in there." That's what I did. I ignored it. And then it got worse.

Finally, when we were a day away from going to Palm Springs for a vacation, my friend Carol Ware insisted, "You go to your doctor!" So I went to my internist, Dr. Al Oppenheim. He was going to prescribe some stool softeners, but I said, "Do you think there's any possibility that I might have a polyp?"

He said, "Do you think you do?"

I said, "I think this is bad."

He did a rectal exam and didn't feel anything, but he said I should see a gastroenterologist. So I saw a GI doctor while we were in Palm Springs. He did a sigmoidoscopy—he put a rod about twelve inches long into my colon and looked around. He saw nothing. But since I was in so much pain and very anemic, he said, "You've got to see somebody else to get a barium enema when you get home." He said, with a charming accent, "You look'a like'a normal girl, but you're not'a normal girl." That kind of scared me.

As soon as we got back, I went to see a gastroenterologist, Dr. Richard McAuliffe, who agreed that I needed a barium enema. I said, "Can I put it off for a couple of weeks? I've got some seminars to run. IBM is really counting on me!" He advised me to get the test as soon as possible.

I ran the seminar on Tuesday, Wednesday, and Thursday. I kept having to sit down and put my feet up because I felt so much discomfort in my abdomen. On Friday I had the barium. Dr. McAuliffe called at the end of the day and said, "You either have a tumor or some very enlarged polyps. Come see me on Monday morning and we'll talk about it."

Friday night I thought everything was okay. Monday morning, June 8, Dr. McAuliffe told me I had colon cancer. I'd have to have surgery and I'd have to have it soon. I immediately went into my businesswoman role, asking smart questions like, "How big is it?" and "How serious is it?" I wanted information so I could examine this new problem the same logical way I always examined problems. Underneath, I was scared to death.

I was scheduled to conduct another seminar over the next three days, so I spent most of Monday evening preparing my colleague, Oren Harari, to teach my part. Craig couldn't believe it. He said, "You just found out you have cancer, and you're working when I'd rather be with you." Here I was, putting work first as usual.

The next day, Tuesday, I saw the colorectal surgeon. I asked, "Is there any chance at all that this is not cancer?" He said, "I guess there is one chance in a million," and then he quoted the statistics: 156,000 people are diagnosed with colon cancer and 58,300 people die of it every year. Craig and I were shocked . . . we had gone from constipation to cancer so quickly.

We scheduled the surgery for Friday, June 12, which was also the thirteenth anniversary of the date Craig and I met. We thought, "Maybe that will bring us luck." It hadn't occurred to us at the time that there might be any metastases.

Immediately after surgery, the first thing I remember was, "Hurt! Hurt!" The anesthesiologist had assured me, "We won't let you hurt," and I was yelling, "Hurt! Hurt!" What he had failed to do was explain that it takes a while to determine what dose of painkiller you need after the anesthesia wears off. But instead a nurse came up and said, as if to a child, "Well, of course you hurt, honey, you just had surgery!"

When the anesthesiologist came over to see how I was doing, I grabbed his smock and asked, "What happened?" He started to say that the surgeon would talk to me after I got back to my room, but I insisted, "I want to know now."

He said, "We couldn't get it all."

I repeated, "I want to know it all, right now."

He said, "Do you want to see the path report?"

I said, "I sure do." And he brought me the pathology report to read—in the recovery room.

Meanwhile, my mother Dottie, Craig, and my friends Brent Ort and Sue Darling were in the waiting room. They saw me being wheeled out of the recovery room reading the pathology report. I think it gave them a sense that everything was going to be all right. That I wasn't going to fall apart. I responded the same way I respond to any other kind of problem: Okay, find out as much as you can, consider your options, figure out a plan of action, try it.

Telling People

The first thing I thought was, "How am I going to tell people? What's the right way to do it?"

It was hard to tell people. I never did learn the right way.

"How are you?"

"Oh, I have cancer, how are you?"

"How are you doing?"

"Not toooo well. I have . . . cancer."

My friend Madeline Cains called from Connecticut while I was preparing Oren to teach my part of the IBM seminar. I didn't have time to talk to her, and I didn't want to tell her quickly. She kept asking, "Tell me why you're having surgery. I want to know. Can't you just take three minutes to tell me?"

I said, "Okay, Madeline, I have cancer, I'll call you later, goodbye."

She broke down. That was the first time I realized that I was responsible for communicating in ways that helped people feel comfortable with me.

There is no right way to tell people. At first I would say, "Look, this is very difficult to say, it's sort of shocking, but I just found out I have cancer. That's all I know for now." I told people I didn't know how serious it was. What else could I say? I didn't really know any more than that.

A few months after my surgery, 1 was working on a project with one of my clients. I told her the truth: "I can't promise deadlines because although you may give me a month to get something done, I may feel good for only four days in all that time." I said, "My cancer is not curable. I'm taking chemotherapy treatments with the hope of reaching remission, but I can't expect myself to perform the way I was able to perform before. I need you to know that there may be a time when I say, 'That's it, I can't do any more,' and it might be right in the middle of the project."

She got a little teary. She said, "We're not going to think about that happening. We're going to think that you will be able to do it and you will enjoy doing it. If there's any problem, then you just need to let me know." She was very caring and that was helpful. Just as she got teary, her assistant came into her office and it was a good excuse for us to change the subject. I was afraid I was going to cry, too.

The truth, gently told, turned out to be the best way for me to give people the news. I think it's impossible to keep such news a secret. People would find out eventually, and then they would talk about me behind my back, so how much privacy would I have? I'd rather have it out in the open so I can be sure people get the correct information. There are some drawbacks, but I think the rewards greatly outweigh the drawbacks.

I think most people who have cancer talk less about it than I do. Some of my new friends with cancer even try to keep it a secret in their families, because "Aunt Tilly" or someone couldn't take it.

At first, it never even entered my mind to consider who to tell and who not to tell. I wanted everybody to know because I needed their care and support. And because I couldn't imagine trying to keep it a secret. I respect my family and friends too much. I would be very upset if one of them had cancer and didn't tell me, didn't give me the opportunity to express my love and to help in some way.

One advantage of people knowing is that help is on the way. One disadvantage is that you lose some of your privacy. When people come over to drop off food, I feel I have to see them. I have to straighten my hair, put on lipstick, hobble to the door, and hope they leave quickly because visiting tires me out. You have to decide if you want this kind of help.

The question of how much to tell people changed for me as the months went on. As I got worse, I found myself thinking, "It's not everybody's business." Then, after I had to have a colostomy in October 1993, I realized I didn't know who knew that I'd had the operation. I didn't know who my family members had told, and I wished I had told them that I wanted to decide who to tell. I thought, "Why couldn't I have gotten cancer of the elbow or the toe—someplace that's not so embarrassing." I know everyone else thought it was good news: "Linda's going to have a colostomy—she's going to be okay!" Well, it was good news that I got a colostomy instead of an ileostomy, which is even more difficult to live with. But I had learned an important lesson: before going into surgery, think about who should be told and how much you want them to know. Then tell your family members before they run off to the phones.

Diana

(Linda's friend and next-door neighbor)

Linda called me on Friday, after she had been to the doctor. She said, "Diana, you're the first person I've called. I just had a physical and there's a tumor in my colon that needs surgery." My first reaction was disbelief—how can a person be so healthy and then the next thing you know they have cancer?

Linda's disease was my first experience with a terminal illness. I was frightened of it. If she could get cancer and die, *I* could get cancer and die. If it could happen to Linda it could happen to *me*. I didn't want to deal with death or cancer, to think that she could die.

It made me aware how precious life is, how we take so much for granted. The doctor says, "You have a malignant tumor," and your whole perspective on life changes. You have to confront life and death. You no longer can look away.

For me, cancer has always been a word not to use because cancer means death. Every time I drive past Marin General Hospital and see "Future Cancer Research Center," I look away and say, "That's for somebody else, not me." But now that I'm so involved with Linda and her cancer I've changed from being frightened to being much more interested. I want to know how she feels, I want to understand the process, I want to know more about cancer than I did before. I'm learning that I'm strong, that I can handle somebody who has cancer and not be afraid of it.

Linda teaches me something every day. We don't know what the other person is thinking. You have to ask what is going on. What I'm learning about friendship is that the more you see a person, the more you know a person.

The day before she left on a vacation to Hawaii, two months after her cancer was diagnosed, she said, "Would you like to see my new living room furniture?" She showed me the sofa, the ottoman, the chair. Then she said, "I sure hope I'm alive when this living room gets put together. I'll be disappointed if I'm not around to see it. The doctors say I have a fifty-fifty chance of living for five years if the chemo works. But I also have a fifty-fifty chance of dying before the year is up, if it doesn't work. So if it's not going to work, I should be getting deathly sick around the holidays."

I said, "We're not going to think that, Linda. We're going to think about having a Christmas party. We're going to sit around your table and visualize that you're going to be healthy at Christmastime." She said, "Fine."

We vacillate. She vacillates between thinking she's going to make it and thinking she's not. I think that's normal. I took a picture of her and Matt together one Sunday. What I was thinking was, "I want this picture of Linda. She looks so great today."

March

(Linda's mother-in-law)

⌒∞⌒

Linda was more than a daughter-in-law to me. She was the daughter I didn't have.

Our relationship blossomed with Matt's adoption. My husband George and I went down to visit and stayed three years. I was so pleased that Linda was happy to have me with them. She always included me, whether it was shopping in the city or poking around in antique shops for furnishings for their new house. It always impressed me that she always knew exactly what she wanted.

When Craig phoned to tell me Linda had colon cancer and that it was peppered throughout her vital organs, my first reaction was anger with the doctors. I knew she'd been taking good care of herself and going in for annual checkups. So I thought, "How could that be possible?" Her pamphlets said the usual symptoms were constipation and polyps. I thought they would have given her a barium enema somewhere along the way. That's how they finally found out, the barium test. It's such a simple thing.

My husband said, "Doctors are only people, you know." I said, "I know, but they have experience." Maybe you have to blame someone when something like this happens. We can go to the moon, but we still can't diagnose cancer early enough.

I think attitude has a lot to do with how you cope with illness. Linda wanted to have as much time as possible with Matt, and that determination helped her last as long as she did.

The extended period of Linda's illness brought us all closer together. I'd had cervical cancer at age thirty, and I cried for my then young children. I had lost both my parents by age ten, and now I wanted to be with Linda and Craig, and most of all with Matt. It was an honor to be asked.

Letting People Help

❧

I remember offering to help when other people were sick, even if I didn't know them well. I was always disappointed because they never asked, so I'd send flowers and never know what else I could have done. So I decided I was going to take people seriously when they said they wanted to help.

We went to back-to-school night at Matt's school and everybody kept saying, "You look so good!" I was embarrassed that I looked so good because these people had been bringing meals over to my house and baby-sitting my son. I felt guilty for asking for their help.

I've always felt guilty about overdramatizing illnesses. I never wanted people to think I was a hypochondriac. I don't want people to think I'm taking advantage of them. So I felt guilty because my mother and my mother-in-law were staying with me instead of going out having fun. One day I told my mom, "Why don't you and Mom Mukai think about when you would like to go home? Craig and I will send you home. You can play bridge with your friends for a week, catch up on your mail, water your plants, and Mom Mukai can do the same." My mom said, "Okay." And as soon as she said "Okay," I wanted to say, "No, stay with me until it's over."

It's amazing how many people have shown they cared. Even people we didn't know that well have offered to help. But I had to learn how to accept their help—and sometimes, how to ask for it.

Some people help me by being available to talk. I can call Diana and say, "I've got to talk right now," and usually she is right there, ready to listen. She challenges me, asking questions that help me to another level of understanding. Some friends, especially Sue and Madeline, help me understand my feelings by telling me what their perceptions are. Other friends stay in constant touch to see if there is anything they can do.

Sometimes I ask a friend to return telephone calls for me, letting people know how I am. I get a few cards and letters each day, some with clipped-out articles from people who've heard about somebody who has been treated by something that's worked. I don't have time to research them all, but I appreciate the concern.

My half sister Susan stays on top of cancer research for me. If she reads a newspaper or a magazine about a new finding, she calls the company or hospital for more information. She copies articles from medical journals and sends them to me. When something came out about a new drug from Bristol-Myers, she got a copy of the journal article. Then she called Bristol-Myers, the Food and Drug Administration, and the National Cancer Institute to find out more. She's a real angel.

It's moving to have people you don't know come by, bringing meals, tapes, reading materials. One couple from my church, people I didn't even know, showed up at the door with food they'd already cooked and frozen, to put into our freezer. It was totally unexpected and wonderful. It's wonderful to get cards in the mail: "I don't think we've met at church but I wanted you to know you're in my prayers." These people didn't have to go out of their way to buy a card or a gift, prepare a meal, drive all the way over to my house. It reinforces my hope for mankind to know that there are still people out there—a lot of them—with enormous hearts.

I learned that people can help in lots of ways, if I let them. I was too tired to clean up after Thanksgiving, so I let my mother do it. Normally I would have said, "Mom, wait, I'll do it later." I couldn't let myself feel guilty about it. And I knew that Mom wanted to help in any way she could.

My friend Carol Ware is so gutsy and funny and cares so much. She wanted to do something special. She asked me, "Who's your favorite actor?"

I said, "It's hard to choose, but one of my all-time favorites is Gregory Peck." Carol called the library for his address and wrote to him, telling him I was a fan who had cancer. She asked him to send me an autograph or a picture. But he wrote me a letter! It even looks as if he typed it himself on an old manual typewriter. I do believe that he is a man of character.

My mother-in-law March and my father-in-law George know how important it is for me to maintain or gain weight, so they buy or fix my favorite foods to encourage me to eat. George sends me candy, hand-selected, to delight me.

I really appreciate cards and letters. I don't think people realize that their words mean even more than flowers and gifts. In just one week, I got three cards that touched me and made me cry. One was from a friend I hadn't heard from in a long time. He said, "I've had this card for several months but I haven't sent it because I was waiting to come up with some pearls of wisdom. Since I never came up with any, I want to send it anyway with my best wishes and prayers."

375 NORTH CAROLWOOD DRIVE
LOS ANGLES, CALIFORNAI 90077

June 16, 1992

Ms. Linda Mukai
c/o Ms. Carol Ware
21 Tollridge Court
San Mateo, CA 94402

Dear Linda,

Here's a word of encouragement and
support from an old friend.

I trust that you have come through
your surgery in fine shape, that the
worst is behind you, and all will
be well.

I'm pulling for you. Keep your
spirits up.

Most sincerely,

Gregory Peck

Inside Me, Outside World

❧

I feel as if I'm monitoring the world from a different point of view.

Sue and I found a lot of humor in my situation at first. I had cancer and I felt very apart from the world. But I didn't look sick, I looked fine. And I felt feisty.

Before my first surgery, I wanted to get my "affairs" in order, in case I didn't survive. Sue and I went to the bank to pick up my will so my attorney could update it.

While we were in the bank, Sue and I were kept waiting more than fifteen minutes at the safe-deposit box window. The woman at the next teller's window kept saying, "I'll be there in just a minute," but her line kept going and going, and she didn't come over to us. I said, "Sue, this is ridiculous. I have cancer! I want service and I want it now!"

Sue said, "Let's get some T-shirts made: 'Fast Service, I have cancer.'" I thought it was a great idea, a wonderful business opportunity. There are Crazy Shirts and Loco Shirts, so why not T-shirts for sick people that say, "I have cancer, please let me go first."

Even with the American Disabilities Act, there is no accommodation made for sick and disabled people in public places such as banks, restaurants, and food stores. Maybe there is a wheelchair ramp or signs in Braille, but there's no special line that says,

"People who need fast service because they're sick or have a physical impairment, wait here." I thought about the people I've darted in front of in the grocery store and wondered how often I might have caused a sick person to wait.

In the fall of 1992, I flew to Ohio for business. I had to change planes in Chicago, and there were thirty gates between the planes. So I went up to one of those electric cart drivers and said, "I'm a cancer patient. Can you take me to gate 32?"

He said, "Did you reserve a space?"

I said, "No, but I didn't know it was going to be this far."

He said, "Go ahead and sit down in the cart and we'll see what happens."

As it turned out, he was able to take me to my gate. So there we were, traveling through the airport, with people streaming up and down, tooting our little horn to get them out of the way, and I felt it was a metaphor for my whole situation: "I'm speeding ahead to something that you people are walking toward." People moved out of our way, but they never looked at us. I thought, "One out of three of you folks may have cancer right now or are going to get it, and you're walking around as if your life is fine." That was frightening because I had been one of those people before.

A few months later, a new client called to ask if I could conduct some seminars from April through June. I said, "I can't commit," and told her why. She dropped me like a bag of beans as soon as she heard. I got the impression that she thought, "We don't want anybody hanging around with cancer."

When I cut my hair because it was thinning out, people responded in an odd way: "You cut your hair and you're tan and you look great." The unspoken message seemed to be, "I'm no longer scared when I look at you."

Sometimes people don't think before they talk. I was pulling into the Safeway parking lot on the day of a chemo treatment, and I felt tired and nauseous. I pulled into the handicapped parking spot, put my handicap card in the window, and got out of the car. A woman came up to me and said, "You shouldn't park there because you can get a citation." I looked her right in the eye and said, "You don't have to worry about a citation if you have cancer and you have a handicap card." And she said, "Oh, I just didn't want you to get a citation." What business of hers was it that I parked there? And even after telling her I had cancer, her best comeback was, "I didn't want you to get a citation." She could have said, "Gee, I'm sorry, I hope you'll be all right," or something like that. Looking back, I realize I probably scared her so much she couldn't think of a nice reply. I should have just thanked her, pointed at the card, and gone about my business.

People don't need to protect me. I took a cake to Matt's school one day when it was raining. I was holding an umbrella over the cake and wearing a hat to protect myself. One of the children said, "Mrs. Mukai, why are you wearing a hat?" A worried mother immediately jumped in with, "You don't need to ask her why she's wearing a hat." She must have thought I didn't have any hair. I leaned over to the little girl and said, "I'm wearing a hat because it's raining." Then I took the hat off and out bounced my short, curly locks.

A few weeks after the cancer was diagnosed, a friend called to ask if I could speak at her women's program. I said, "I can't do it. I just learned I have cancer," and I gave her the name of someone else she could call.

She said, "Oh, sorry to hear that and thanks for the name." Months later, she called again and said, "I've felt so guilty for not calling you. We thought maybe we'd try and get together with you, set a date to have dinner."

I explained that it was almost impossible for me to set a date for dinner. Because of my reactions to chemo, I never know how I'm going to feel each evening. I told her that I'd rather that they call spontaneously and say, "We're going out to dinner, do you want to go?"

She said, "Oh, well, good, I was feeling guilty about that and that's fine, we'll do that."

I said, "Thanks for calling," and we hung up. That call was for her. She got her guilt taken care of. Now there's no more obligation. She felt a lot better. I didn't feel any better. I didn't feel better at all. I felt angry. I didn't want her to call again. She couldn't handle it and it's hard for me to handle people who can't handle it.

One cute thing happened when I was in the hospital in late 1993. One of the class moms who had done a lot of work to organize meals and childcare for us left a message on our home phone asking what time somebody could deliver food. I'm sure she was expecting a call back from Craig or one of our moms. But I was feeling pretty good so I called her from the hospital. I said, "Hi, Stephanie, it's Linda Mukai." She was shocked, as if she were hearing a voice from the grave. "Linda, my God, you're calling me!" It was as if she felt special that I would call her myself. I just wanted to thank her for doing all the organizing, to tell her I really appreciated it.

July 18, 1992

Hi, Janis,

It's 1:32 a.m. on Saturday, July 18. I can't sleep. I have so much on my mind.

Yesterday, I had my fourth chemo treatment. I'm really tired, and it's a strange kind of tired, an extreme fatigue. I almost collapsed walking down the hall. Just sitting here in my office I'm so overcome with fatigue that it feels as if every cell in my body is sinking, sinking, sinking. That makes me feel depressed. I want to be able to do things, but all I can do is lie around and watch the political conventions and read the newspaper.

I got more bad news Thursday night. My dad also has colon cancer. It was shocking. I guess some of my symptoms sounded familiar so he went in for a barium and they found an obstruction that looks like a tumor. He goes in for a colonoscopy and biopsy on Friday so we'll know more then, but his doctor is pretty sure it's cancer. Here he is, almost sixty-eight years old, and here I am, forty-six, and we're both growing tumors at the same time.

I can't help but think about what all this must be like for the rest of our family. My stepmother Bobbie, and Lisa and Susan, my half sisters, must be in shock. Lisa and Susan should probably see their doctors—they might be at high risk for colon cancer.

I always thought my dad would live into his late eighties. I don't want to lose him; I need him now. I can't help wondering which one of us is worse, which of us will be there when the other dies, or whether we'll both be too sick even to see each other.

I keep trying to relax, but it's difficult, even though I'm using my relaxation tapes. I lie in bed, lie there and lie there, and try not to think about the fact that I have cancer and don't know how long I'm going to live.

Craig said something interesting the other day. He said, "Hope is just another word for denial." I'm not sure I agree with that. I can hope for a longer life, without denying that I have a very, very, very serious illness.

What I keep wondering is whether this is just the beginning of feeling worse and worse and finally fading out? I have a lot to do before that. But all the things I was going to do in the next couple of weeks keep coming off my calendar because I'm not going to be able to do them. How am I ever going to finish everything on my life's "To Do" list?

We were talking about going to Hawaii from August 1 through the 16th. I don't know if I'll be able to go. I'll be off the chemo for those two weeks, but I know I'll still be tired. I wish I knew whether the chemo was doing any good. I wonder if I'm wasting my good times with this incredible lethargy.

My friends have been wonderful, but they can't give me what I need. It seems as if everyone is taking my illness so calmly. Are they reflecting my behavior? Trying to be strong for me? Maybe they're confused about what to say or do. I just can't understand why they don't seem upset. What I need is nurturing. I need someone to help me cry. To cry with me. But I guess I haven't let anyone know how I feel, and what I need. I've been making shockingly morbid jokes. I've been matter-of-fact in the way I talk about having cancer. No emotion. I don't know whether I'm in denial or I've already moved into acceptance. Maybe I'm still in shock.

Sometimes I feel as if I'm the lead character in a play: "This isn't really happening to me." All the other actors are saying their lines, but they're not really involved because none of this is real. And sometimes I feel as if I'm standing apart from everything that's going on, watching but not participating.

Today I was supposed to have a telephone conference with a client at three o'clock. I forgot to call her. I came home from the doctor's office and fell asleep. That's not like me. I don't forget things like that.

I don't know if I really want to keep working. On the one hand, I'm tickled to death at the idea of doing some of the projects I've got lined up. On the other, I can't seem to drag my legs and arms into the fray. I can't even seem to write a letter to one client who wants it right away. I keep wanting to put things off. I'm just too, too tired. But I don't want to sleep my life away, whatever is left of it.

I probably need some therapy right now. I'm too tired to get it. I've got names of some people who could help me, but I haven't made the effort to call. I can't remember where I put the phone numbers and I don't want to go look for them because I'm too tired.

Well, now it's 2:01. Time to take another sleeping pill and get serious about trying to sleep. Thanks for listening. Goodnight, Janis.

Sue

(Linda's assistant and close friend)

I think it's important to learn as much about the illness as possible, so you can understand what's happening. That's what has been so wonderful with Linda, since I didn't do it with my mother, who died of cancer several years ago. In the case of my mother, it happened so fast we had very little time to talk about the cancer and our feelings for each other. Linda and I talk about it. I ask questions. I understand what's happening in the moment to her, what her body is doing, what it's fighting. We have a wonderful relationship.

People do treat people who are ill differently. I can tell that some people are afraid to deal with her. They don't want to come to see her. They don't want to deal with it in themselves. People are dealing with their own fears: "What if this were to happen to me—there's a woman who's vivacious, talented, and full of energy. And this is happening to her. Maybe it could happen to me!"

One lesson Linda is having to learn is patience. Here's a woman who was in control of her life and now everything has changed. One day we took a walk in the hospital. She wanted to go down a long hallway. I suggested politely, "Don't you think that this is enough?"

She said, "No, I'd really like to go down this hallway."

"You don't think this is enough?"

"No, I'm not tired. Let's go down this hall."

I was getting concerned because it was a long way for her on her first day up. I could see that the energy had drained out of her, but I wasn't assertive enough to say, "No, I really feel this is too much to do right now," and besides, she wouldn't have listened to me anyway. These kinds of things annoy me, but they make me realize that I'm projecting my own issues onto her.

It is devastating to me to think of Matt growing up without a mother. One day Linda told me that that was one of her fears. She has so much to offer as a mother.

I've learned that life is change. Linda may have to go to the doctor, or she may have to go get an X-ray, and I have to change my work day, or my personal day. That was difficult at first. I kept thinking, "I have all this stuff piling up on my desk, not getting done." Then one day, it hit me. Changes in our lives are always difficult. We have to accept the changes and move with them. So what if this or that doesn't get done on my desk? What's really important here?

Before she went on her trip to Hawaii, I ordered a wheelchair from the airlines. I wasn't going to tell her until we got to the airport because I thought, "She'll never go in a wheelchair." But I knew she needed her energy for the trip.

Then she called me and said, "You know, I have this great idea. Why don't we get me a wheelchair?" I thought, "That's great!" I think we're both learning.

Janis

In the middle of September, three months after we began this book, Linda called me from her car phone. She was jubilant. Her CEA (the Carcinoma Embryonic Antigen count that indicates tumor activity), which was 400 in June, was down to 25 (normal is 0–2.5). The tumor growth had slowed, and her doctor had carefully implied that it might be all right to talk in terms of years instead of months. Of course, Linda was jubilant. *Hope!* had reared its head, and it was beautiful. "A couple of months ago I wouldn't have thought that one or two years was a very long time," she said, "but now it seems like forever."

I was very happy for Linda, and I told her so. What I did not say was that I was also afraid for her. I didn't want her to begin living her life again only to wake to a wallop on the side of the head.

What I wanted was for Robert Young to step out of the mist, stethoscope in hand, a beatific smile on his handsome face: "You're cured! A miracle, but you're cured!" But I knew that's not the way it goes with cancer and Linda knew that, too. So what's wrong with being jubilant? You have to live moment to moment when you might die out of time. Couldn't I let a particular moment be jubilant?

I had been working with Linda for only three months, and I had already learned some important lessons. One is that this business of dying is far more complicated than I had realized. A few weeks before Linda's good news, my friend Jay died, also of cancer. I had gone to their house on Saturday with a chicken so Jay's wife Bette could make him some matzoh-ball soup, but I found only a note on the door saying they'd taken Jay to the hospital. By Monday they'd discovered that the cancer was in his liver and there was nothing to be done.

I stopped by the hospital on Wednesday. Bette was on the phone, giving directions from the airport for Jay's brother and cousin who were arriving on Thursday. I was struck by the way illness interrupts people's lives. I wondered how sick someone has to be before you drop everything and buy a plane ticket. Does the sick person have to be dying? Isn't the idea to see the person *before* they are at the point of dying? Before they die? At what point is there no decision—you just go?

I remembered Linda wondering aloud whether she and her father would be able to be together if one or the other of them reached their last days. Whether the person who was not yet dying would be well enough to travel. I think I would want people to visit me while I was still well enough to enjoy them. I realize, though, that you don't have to enjoy people; you just want them to be there.

At the hospital with Bette and Jay, I felt like a voyeur, like the time my daughter Jennifer and I accidentally walked past the yellow ribbon that blocked off downtown San Anselmo after a flood. We walked around gaping at the devastation until someone stopped us and we turned back, embarrassed by the realization that we had been trespassing on other people's tragedies.

That's how I sometimes feel with Linda, like a voyeur, wanting to help, wanting to watch what is happening, but also wanting to stay back, hating my intense feeling of relief that this is her cancer, not mine.

By October, a month after the good news about her CEA count, it was clear that Linda was not going to die before the holidays as the doctors had predicted when the cancer was first diagnosed. She was working and she felt fairly well, although the chemo made her very tired. As her condition improved, my initial sense of urgency to finish this book diminished, and my attention wavered. I had an envelope of tapes that needed transcription, a pile of transcripts to work on. But I kept putting the work aside in favor of projects with more immediate payoffs.

But I was fooling myself. This was not the end, only the middle passage. A time bomb was still ticking inside Linda's body. I had to keep reminding myself that the payoff for this project was there, only not easy to see: the chance to do something for someone else, no strings. People seldom get those kinds of chances. I forced myself back to work.

And the lessons keep coming. I think about the trust we place in our doctors. Linda's mother-in-law March spoke of her frustration that the disease was not caught earlier, and I, too, wonder why Linda's doctors didn't warn her, why they didn't listen more carefully to her symptoms—although Linda herself said that she never told them enough about her symptoms. I don't care. They should have guessed. Someone should have guessed. Someone has to be responsible. Someone has to be at fault.

But I can see that the ultimate responsibility lies with each of us. We have to pay attention to our own bodies, to notice changes, to speak up when we think something might be wrong. We have to understand that doctors must walk a fine line between taking too much action too soon and not taking enough too late. We also have to understand that we know our own bodies best. If we think something is wrong, we should not take, "Let's wait and see," for an answer. We shouldn't worry, as my mother does, about offending our doctors by getting another opinion. Doctors don't always know best. It really is up to each of us to direct our own health care. We must learn how to do that, and I'm still not sure where we get the tools to do it well.

TREATMENT

A Crash Course
in Cancer Treatment

*When Audrey Hepburn died so soon after surgery for colon cancer, I
thought, "Gee, her cancer must have been a lot worse than mine."
I wanted facts. But they only reported on her movies and her
humanitarian activities. I'm sure her family considered her
illness private, but it might be helpful for those of us who are
suffering from this disease to know more. Lives might be
saved by informing people who have colon cancer symptoms
to see their doctors. But I guess it's not newsworthy.*

Dr. Spivack, my oncologist, told me he kept up on all the current
cancer research and if at any time he felt he couldn't help me anymore, he would put me in touch with the right person or place.
But then I thought, "Well that's wonderful, but he doesn't spend
all his time thinking about Linda Mukai. He's got a lot of other
patients to think about."

I realized that it was my job to stay on top of my disease, to
learn what I could about various medical treatments and alternative approaches. I consulted with three more oncologists, all of
whom agreed with Dr. Spivack's treatment plan.

One of the oncologists I spoke with told me about a doctor
in Washington, D.C., who does aggressive cancer surgery to try
to get every cancer cell out of the body. But evidently I wasn't a

candidate because my cancer was too advanced. The surgery might catch one cell here and there, but some would still spread to another place. I hoped the doctor might take me, but Dr. Spivack said I should wait and see how I responded to chemotherapy.

I read a research article by a doctor at the University of California at Los Angeles that mentioned generally poor results from the kind of chemotherapy I was receiving. I felt very confused, so I continued to gather information. In September 1993, I read about a new drug that Bristol-Myers was working on. Their results on mice had been impressive—they had been able to cure well-established metastatic disease. But human trials hadn't even begun.

I called Bristol-Myers and said I would be glad to be the first name on their waiting list for experimentation with this new drug. They took my name and number, but they said it would be at least six months before they got FDA approval for trials. It was frustrating to know that there was something out there that might help, yet not be able to get it.

I try to limit my readings on cancer research to things that have some scientific evidence. If I see something in the newspaper that I want to know more about, I check to see where it came from. I'll fax it off to Susan, who looks into it further. Sometimes I also read about alternative approaches. I don't want to miss anything that might be useful.

At the beginning, I looked everywhere for information about cancer and about having a life-threatening illness. I must have read five or six books about cancer and ten to fifteen books about other issues: staying positive, meditation, and spirituality.

Educating myself gives me questions for my doctors and allows me to make the best choices. It helps me feel that I'm doing everything I can for myself. If I'm really keeping up, I can respond intelligently to friends who call to tell me about a new miracle cure they've just heard about.

After the first few months, I knew the questions to ask to determine very quickly whether I wanted to know more about something. For example, I hadn't known that treatments for breast cancer might not work for colon cancer. I had thought that chemo was chemo, but I learned that every kind of cancer has its own kind of chemotherapy, and that some people have radiation and some don't.

I bought a general encyclopedia of cancer, *Everyone's Guide to Cancer Therapy*, by Malin Dollinger, M.D., Ernest H. Rosenbaum, M.D., and Greg Cable, and it's been extremely helpful. I keep it close to me because I'm constantly looking something up.

There's a twenty-four-hour-a-day toll-free number, 1-800-FOR-CANCER, where I can get answers to my questions over the phone from the National Cancer Institute. They'll send out articles from journals, lists of all the clinical trials being run in the United States on a disease, and more. It saves time; I don't have to go to a library to get information. And it's free. There are also on-line resources. One is called MedLine. I can sit down at a computer terminal at the University of California Medical Center in San Francisco, ask about Taxol, and get a list of all the articles that have been published about that drug. In some cases MedLine has abstracts, so I can skim the articles instead of looking them up. It's also free.

Taking Care of Myself

 ◁◈▷

*I feel as if every day I live is a lifetime. I wake in the
morning and I am born and I go to bed at night and I die.
I'm the one who's in charge of what happens in between.*

As soon as I found out I had cancer, I realized that the most important things for me to do were to enjoy my family, take care of myself, and try to make the most of every moment. When I'm involved in something I enjoy, I feel better, and the cancer moves to the back of my mind. In fact, several months after the cancer was diagnosed, I thought, "If it weren't for all the doctor appointments, I'd be having the time of my life."

While I was on a chemo break in October 1992, Craig and I went to Sedona, Arizona, for ten days. We had a wonderful time. It was the best vacation the two of us have ever had together. One day we drove all the way up to Monument Valley, just across the Utah border, then southeast to Canyon de Chelly, and back to Sedona. It was a seventeen-hour day, in and out of the car, looking at beautiful things, taking pictures, talking, listening to music and books on tape.

I wanted to do things that are considered healing in Arizona. There are several vortexes there, supposedly areas of immense energy. We climbed halfway up Bell Rock and found a little cave. I sat in there thinking positive thoughts and pulling the energy towards my body saying, "If there's any healing here, come to me." We went to a chapel built into one of the canyons and I said a prayer for myself and my dad. Every day I wore the amethyst amulet that Madeline had given me. I felt great. I had no nausea. No pain. I felt grounded out there in God's country.

The next April we went to Scottsdale and spent several days with my dad, my stepmother Bobbie, and my sister Susan. When we left for the airport, Dad and I hugged and he said, "Do you know what? We never mentioned the 'C' word the whole time." It was a normal family get-together. We talked about world affairs, weather, people and things. Cancer never came up!

Being at the resort in Scottsdale, meeting people, sitting around the pool with other parents and their children and not mentioning I had cancer was wonderful. I thought, "It's funny, those people don't know why I have this big scar on my stomach, and they don't need to know." Not telling them made me feel more normal, like a well person. It gave me the freedom not to endure their pain, not to have to relieve their fear.

During the first months after the initial surgery, I had to learn how best to use my time. I took on a few business projects. I worked on decorating the house and designing the landscaping for our front yard. I wanted to create a nicer space because I knew I was going to be at home a lot more. I began to consider myself semiretired. I learned not to waste my time and energy washing dishes and making beds. Not to worry if Matt's room was messy.

I had to recognize that I no longer had the energy or the stamina to carry on life as usual. The next time I was in the hospital I learned to ask the nurses to put a sign on the door asking visitors to stay only five or ten minutes, so I could get the rest I needed. As loving and caring as they were, my visitors didn't realize how tiring their visits were for me. Talking to people is a lot of work. I didn't know that before; talking to people had been my hobby.

I learned to take charge, to set clearer boundaries and expectations. When a client and I were working out a project schedule, I said, "I can only work two days a week. My fee is this, and I want to be paid within ten days of invoice." I had never been quite that assertive before.

I learned that life is too short for doing things that other people wanted me to do but that I didn't want to do myself. Sometimes I've handled those situations well, and sometimes I've been rude. One day, Craig and I went to a Planning Commission meeting because a neighbor was trying to stop our son's school from using its baseball field, which was next to his property. Craig made a statement in favor of the school and our neighbor's appeal was denied. The neighbor called the next night and said, "We'd like to get together with you, have a glass of wine, and discuss the ball field and our neighborly relationship."

I said, "Look, I really don't want to have a glass of wine and discuss our neighborly relationship. The ball field issue is closed, and it has nothing to do with our relationship. Let's let it drop." It was a brusque response. I should have thanked him for his invitation and politely declined. Learning to say no graciously can be difficult for me now.

Sometimes it's hard to remember to take care of yourself because your life doesn't stop when you get cancer. Whatever was going on for you before you were diagnosed is still there. People don't say, "She's got cancer, let's clear up our personal problems so she won't have any stress." Those are pipe dreams. Of course, that's what I want people to do. I want them to say, "She's sick, let's not fight." But that's not the way it is. I'm still a mom, and I'm still a wife. I still play referee, harmonizer, peacekeeper, and gatekeeper between husband and child. I still insert myself into a lot of family situations that Craig's asked me to keep out of.

Boys and dads argue. I grew up in a yelling household, and it's
scary for me. It doesn't matter how badly I'm feeling, if there's
something going on between Craig and Matt, I jump out of bed
with some kind of miraculous energy. I forget I'm lying here
dying of cancer and I'm off and running, playing the mom role to
its fullest extent. Craig always says, "Give it up. Let me take care
of it," but I can't. Sometimes I know I'm the only person who's
going to be able to take care of it as well or as quickly: "Super
Mom. Rescue squad coming out." Things seem to escalate if I
don't insert myself. That's my final worry, that I won't be here to
do that. But if I do insert myself, things escalate for me. I'm supposed to be in a nonstressful environment.

I told Craig that I knew I was going to have to set boundaries
to take care of myself. I said, "I do not want to hear yelling and
screaming in the house." But I still don't know how to let it go. I
guess that's just part of my own stubbornness. If I think I'm right
about something, I'm not going to let go of it.

I also realized that I had to quit expecting so much from
myself. In December 1992, I got some good news—the cancer
growth had slowed. The next day I was irritable all day. I was
angry with Matt, angry with Mom, angry with Craig, angry with
Sue. Nobody could please me. I told my psychiatrist about it and
asked, "Why am I acting this way when it was good news?"

She said, "Is it good news?"

I said, "What a silly question. Of course it's good news."

"Think about it. What does it mean if you're better? What's
that going to require of you?" She said, "When you put excel-
lence on a scale between 0 and 100, your problem is that if you
don't hit 100, you think you've hit 0. You've got to find a place in
the 50-to-70 percent category where you can be satisfied."

It all became clear. I was afraid that people were going to
expect me to do as much—and do it as well—as I did before. *I*
was going to expect more of myself, too. So I was grumpy when
my mother said we should go to the grocery store, when Craig
asked me to help bring in the groceries, when Matt left toys and
clothes on the floor for me to clean up. I didn't feel like doing any
of those things. Even though my blood counts and scans had
improved, I didn't feel any better. I was still on chemo and I still
had cancer.

I told everybody, "Please don't expect more from me just because my scans show I'm better. I still don't feel well and I have to rest just as much." The surprise was they really didn't expect more from me. I had put the whole burden on myself.

Taking care of myself sometimes means doing things I don't want to do, like eating. I have to eat. If I can't eat, I drink Ensure, a high-calorie nutritional product. It isn't a gourmet meal, but it helps me maintain weight and that's very important. I need to weigh about ten pounds more than normal because I never know when I'm going to get sick and lose ten pounds in a few days. I never know when I'm going to have emergency surgery and drop weight fast.

It's also important for me to get outside, to breathe fresh air, to let the sun's rays touch my skin. It lifts my depression. It's so easy to stay in bed all day and feel sorry for myself. Sometimes I tell myself that I'm taking care of myself by staying in bed, but when I force myself to get up, take a shower, and get dressed, I'm amazed at how much energy I have. Suddenly I'm in the mood to do something, maybe go out for lunch with a friend. I need to test how much I am capable of doing and push a little.

One day Craig came home saying, "Surprise, surprise, something for you!" And he rolled a wheelchair into the bedroom. I started to cry. I had been in bed the whole week feeling sick and fatigued, and I thought he was trying to tell me to get up—when all he was trying to do was make it easier for me to get out. But I became defensive, and I asked him to take it back.

Several months later, when I got out of the hospital after the colostomy, I said, "Let's rent that wheelchair. You were right, it will give me more freedom." I wanted to go shopping because I needed clothes without waistbands, but I didn't have the energy to walk through a shopping mall.

I'm probably best at boundary setting, deciding how much I'm going to do with people or on the phone or with doctors, how much advice I'm going to take, what I'm willing to do for myself. A lot of people in my cancer support group are not only on chemo and radiation and going to various support groups and psychologists or psychiatrists, but they're also going to acupuncture, acupressure, massage, and herbalist appointments. There are so many things you can do. I could program myself to do nothing but cancer treatment all day. I could become a Zen master while I'm working on my cancer! I feel guilty sometimes when I think, "It's been a week since I've done any of those things. Does that mean I'm not taking care of myself?" But then my shrink said, "If you do more of that stuff, you might not feel well enough for the treatments and surgery you need." It still comes back to boundary setting—how much advice, and what advice, to take.

Checking out the Alternatives

God only knows what will work—you may find out you can cure cancer by eating spider legs. A friend who had read something about carrot juice and cancer gave me a bottle of carrot juice. The next day the bottle was so swollen up it almost exploded. Craig said, "I'm glad you didn't take that; you might have been dead today." I haven't figured out how to write a thank-you note to that friend yet. It's one of those times when you thank people for their intent.

I get a massage every week. I don't know if it has an impact on cancer, but it makes me feel good for an hour or so. Sometimes during the massage I just lie there and enjoy it, other times I like to chat with the massage therapist, and sometimes I meditate or visualize. Meditation helps me relax. When I'm meditating I'm on a different plane. It's like floating, pulling away from reality. I can do whatever I want, and I can know everything. I think it's healthy because it gives me a feeling that I have some control.

I have an active imagination so I enjoy visualizing myself healing and feeling well. Sometimes I visualize a cancer cell being attacked by the chemo, the cell splitting into tiny parts and the white cells rushing in to grab the pieces and carry them away to be disposed of. I feel myself working magic on my body.

Meditation and imagery are very powerful. I can reduce my pain by using them. But when I am very frightened, I find it difficult to meditate. I'm told that if I practice more, I will be able to use meditation to reduce my fear, so I try to practice at least twice a day.

My friend Judy Hulka and I went to see Bill Moyers when he spoke in San Francisco to introduce the PBS series "Healing and the Mind," which was based on his book. Three thousand people were there.

Moyers said, "The first thing I want you to know is that I am not proposing anyone stop Western medical treatment—if you need chemo, get chemo. What we're talking about is healing, and healing to me means healing the mind, not necessarily just the body; it doesn't mean curing."

He said that people are feeling more and more comfortable using alternative health care techniques. In fact, more money is actually being spent on alternative methods than on ordinary Western medicine.

He also said that few patients using alternative therapies tell their doctors that they're using them. That's true in my case. Dr. Spivack has no idea that I take certain vitamins, that I take an aspirin every day. I haven't told him and he hasn't asked. If he knew, I think he'd say something like, "That's fine, but don't expect anything." He's a medicine man.

Some alternative treatments can be very expensive: vitamins, herbs, massage, acupuncture, chiropractic, and psychotherapy don't come cheap. But other alternatives, such as support groups, yoga, meditation, visualization, exercise, and a healthy diet usually cost nothing or very little.

In October 1993, Craig and I spent a week at a cancer "retreat," Commonweal, in Bolinas, California. It's a place where cancer patients—and their significant others or caregivers, if they wish—come for a week.

In the fifteen years Craig and I have been married, we have had two vacations that were the high points of our lives together. One was the vacation we took in Arizona in 1992, after my first chemo break, and the second was the week we spent at Commonweal.

I didn't expect Commonweal to be an experience for us as a couple. We were going with the idea that we each wanted to learn more about cancer, about treatment, about alternatives, about how other people live and cope each day. We felt there was a lot we could learn about the spiritual aspects of the yoga, relaxation, and meditation techniques they teach. We were on a waiting list for quite a while before we got in. They only take eight people, cancer patients and caregivers, for one week, and they only do it four times a year. There's a fee, but half of the cost is absorbed by Commonweal. They survive with private funding.

The best way to illustrate our Commonweal experience is to describe what happened the very first day. As usual, I wasn't feeling very well when we got up in the morning. But I had packed the night before and I was ready. Craig was dragging his heels. I kept saying, "Get packed, come on, let's go, let's go."

Craig said, "We don't have to be there until 10:30."

I said, "No, no, it starts at 10:00. We're supposed to be there at 9:30 to fill out the paperwork."

He said, "No, it's 10:30."

Of course, we couldn't find the information they had mailed us so that one of us could be proved right and the other wrong, so we continued to argue about it. We finally left home about 9:30. I was overanxious, slightly miffed at Craig and, as usual, concerned that I was going to look bad by showing up late.

It's a long drive from San Anselmo to Bolinas, and it took us a long time to find the place. When we got there, someone said, "This is the administration building. You need to go over to the big house to check in, then come back here to fill out your paperwork." Nobody seemed concerned that we were late, but everyone else was already filling out the paperwork. We were obviously the last ones to arrive.

We hurried over to the other building, rushed in and put our stuff down. A man approached us, said he was glad to meet us, and began telling us about the house. I thought, "The program is going to start, let's go." We finally extracted ourselves and climbed up to our second-floor bedroom. We put our things away in a very small room, with a tiny little bed, and I thought, "This is going to be miserable."

We rushed back to the administration building where we filled out paperwork. Then each participant was called in to a short interview; Craig and I were the last ones. We got to see a timetable, a schedule of activities, and I thought, "There's nothing happening until after 12:00!" Lunch at 12:00, and then nothing until 3:00. I said, "Is there anything happening?"

Waz, the program coordinator who was interviewing us, said, "It's happening right now. This is it." And I thought, "Aha." Our first lesson was "slooooooow down."

At lunch, it seemed as if everybody was more in tune than we were, more settled, slower, more relaxed. I was still anxious. I wanted a formal activity, where we would sit in a circle and find out who everyone was. It wasn't enough to sit down and have lunch with people. I wanted introductions and objectives, all the things I'm used to in a seminar. And that didn't happen. After lunch, Craig and I went up to the bedroom and took a nap. We were exhausted.

At 3:00 the program began. But there were still no introductions, only information about Commonweal, a little history and background. Then we were free again until dinner at 6:00. There we were with all this time to do nothing.

After dinner we finally had a circle where each person told his or her story. That was the purpose, not just an introduction, but a story about why we were there and what kind of cancer we had and so forth. It was very moving. That old line about everybody having a story is really true. Everybody's story was so beautiful. Each person was like a movie star to me, a fascinating character I would get to know during the rest of the week.

One person spoke before me and then I introduced myself. Craig was sitting next to me, so I assumed that he would follow my turn. But one of the men piped up and said, "I'll go next because he doesn't have cancer," pointing at Craig. The facilitator stopped him and said, "No, but he is an integral part of this group. He is a member of the group, not an observer, and he has a story to tell, too. So you can go ahead and introduce yourself if you want to, but we will get back to Craig at some point."

Craig went ahead. And he began to cry. He cried from his first word. It was amazing to me because of all the people in that group, he was the last one I expected to cry. He was the last one *they* expected to cry. He was probably the most moving person in the group. And there was something about what he said that sort of pulled the rest of us together. He told of the love he had for me in such a way that people didn't want him to lose me. You could hear in his voice how much he treasured me. That was my first sign that this was going to be something special for the two of us.

The rest of the week included all kinds of activities—yoga twice a day, massage, sand-tray therapy, individual one-on-one therapy, group therapy. We tackled a lot of cancer issues and whatever else we had on our minds. In a setting like that, people develop such trust they can reveal things they've bottled up for years. One woman told us she had been a victim of incest and she'd only told two people in her lifetime, a teacher, who had told her not to talk like that, and her husband, who had said, "Well, at least you didn't enjoy it." But now she had seven people who loved her and supported her and told her that it didn't matter, she was a pure, clean, innocent human being who was worthy of love and did not deserve the horrible things that had happened to her. I think it was a life-changing event for her.

Commonweal probably has a stated purpose and each person who goes probably sees it in a slightly different way. For me, it was an opportunity to share myself and the horrors and the joys of living after finding out I had this awful disease. It was a discovery that, although the disease is terrible, we all come to a new level of self-knowledge and understanding about what's really important in life. For me, it firmed up my commitment to make each day special. I realized that there were lots of things I could do medically, and through exercise, yoga, meditation, or whatever, to help me through the physical and mental parts of the disease, but the final responsibility for getting the most out of whatever time was left was in my hands. I can't control my cancer, but I have some control over how I'm going to spend my time. That may be the only thing I can control, so I have to get out there and do it.

Oren

(Linda's friend and business associate)

❦

Linda and I met back in 1983 when she hired me to do a seminar at Shaklee Corporation. She was an absolute joy to work with. She would give me the forum to create ideas, and then she would back me up. She knew her strengths, and she didn't have insecurities or ego hangups about being highly visible.

When you work that closely together, either you keep it strictly professional, or you get closer. We got a lot closer, to the point where we were talking about our personal lives. We worked so well together that we started to talk about creating a company.

Our first idea for a company was very ambitious. It would basically have drawn together all the trainers in the Bay Area; we would broker their services for people who needed trainers. We went through meeting after meeting, and we put together a business plan.

Then one day I said, "This idea isn't going to fly, and I don't want to do it." She said, "I don't either." Then she said, "Let's you and I start our own company, a kind of training and consulting company." I said yes, but later I told her that I would have to bail out because I didn't think I could put the energy into it. I started to explain. She said, "Just get to the point. What do you want? What are you trying to tell me?" I told her. She was really unhappy with my decision. That was our most difficult time together.

One thing I learned about Linda the more I got to know her was that she seemed more together than she felt. She churned a lot inside. Several months later, she told me she had gone home from our meeting and couldn't eat, couldn't sleep. It's not that she was angry at me. Mostly she felt, "What am I going to do? I left Shaklee; now the guy I thought I could hang my hat on doesn't have the time."

Eventually, we started working together again. It was mostly her doing. She said, "I'm doing this program. Would you be interested in giving a presentation?" We started developing other programs and doing joint consulting.

It was clear that each of us brought different strengths to a project. She had the ability to listen, to empathize, to create a one-on-one relationship with clients. I barged in there with the intellect, but she would say, "Let's talk. Let me get to know you. Let me get to know your company. Let's talk about your problems." There was always an easiness: "I think I know how to create a solution that is custom-fit for you, and I know the people to bring in to do that." She was fabulous, and the results showed it. Name a large company in the San Francisco Bay Area, and she was probably involved with it at some point.

We did a seminar together as late as August 1993, over a year after her cancer was diagnosed. She put it together, and she sold it. It was a very good one-day seminar. She got tired and had to lie down, but she pulled it off. And they didn't know. They did not know. That seminar was the last thing we did together professionally.

Our relationship changed after she got cancer. I'd still talk a little about my work, and she was always interested. But work seemed so insignificant. Instead, we talked about things like priorities, and family, and values. About what she was doing with Craig and Matt. About more personal things.

It always amazed me how ... I want to use the word "businesslike" ... she approached her illness. I thought, "This woman is systematically going to get the data, she's going to lick this thing, and she's going to do it in an intelligent way." There was no bitterness. I never heard her say, "Why did this happen to me?" Instead, she would talk about how in many ways that last year was the best year of her life in spite of the pain, because of the insights she'd gotten about herself and her family and her friends and her priorities.

Several years earlier, she'd told me that her top priority was her work. There was always something driving her; I never understood exactly what it was. It was beyond work ethic. And that was one of the major shifts she made. I think the lesson she got and would like to convey was that work is important and you should try to make it fulfilling, but at most it's just a part of your life. Sometimes in our frenetic Yuppie society we forget that. We get wrapped up in the minutiae of the work, we think about work all the time, and we don't pay attention to some stuff that is ultimately far more important. In one of his books, Rabbi Harold Kushner wrote something like, "I've never met a man who, on his deathbed, said that he wished he'd spent more time at the office."

I always felt I could have done a lot more for Linda. I was certainly conscious, especially during the last few months, of feeling that I had to be a little careful with her, but I think what she appreciated most was that I was natural. I would say, "Tell me how you're feeling, what's going on?" I would ask about Matt, or Craig. But I also wanted her to have a forum where she could talk about anything, business or music or people, even cheap gossip.

Sometimes when people die, there's a tendency to say, "They were wonderful, they loved animals, and everyone liked them." But there really was something special about Linda. I remember reading that in Japan, in the Samurai times, they would say you can die, but as long as people keep on talking about you, you can live forever. That's why Linda's not really going to die, at least not as long as I'm alive. And I think it's more than simple memory. She touched a lot of people, affected them. That's why she'll always be around.

An Unwelcome Dress Rehearsal

❦

I thought that I would never again see the light of day, never again breathe fresh air. I kept thinking that when my body was ready we would leave, my body and I separately.

One Saturday, after my fourth chemo treatment, I began to feel sick: stomachache, gas, diarrhea, and nausea. On Sunday I called Dr. Spivack and told him I was having a reaction to the chemo. He told me to take certain drugs to minimize the chemo's side effects, keep monitoring myself, and keep checking in.

On Monday I called and said I was still very sick. He said, "Stay on course. Call me tomorrow." Tuesday I didn't call because I thought things were a little better. On Wednesday I talked to his colleague, Dr. Kramer. I remember saying, "I don't feel well at all. Severe, explosive diarrhea. Severe gas pains. I know this isn't normal." But he said it was a normal reaction to chemo and I should continue to use the medication I had been told to use. By this time I was also vomiting. Considering that I hadn't eaten in four days, it seemed odd that I would vomit and have diarrhea.

On Thursday I convinced Dr. Spivack that I was very ill. He told me to go to Marin General Hospital for an X-ray of my abdomen because he was concerned that I might have a blockage.

I was so weak that I collapsed in the entrance to the hospital. They took me to Emergency in a wheelchair, transferred me to a gurney, and then left me there while the nurse called all my doctors to find out whether I should be admitted there or sent by ambulance to U.C. Medical Center where Dr. Spivack had hospital privileges.

I was finally admitted to Marin General because they felt that I was dehydrated and should be attended to without further delay. Dr. Alfred Oppenheim, my internist, and Dr. Richard McAuliffe, my gastroenterologist, came in to examine me. They thought I was having a toxic response to the chemo as well as an infection. They began administering fluids and antibiotics.

By Friday I felt even worse, and by Saturday I was the sickest I had ever been in my life. I needed blood transfusions, so Diana called around for people who would give blood for me. She reached the principal at Matt's school, Sue Maino, and two class moms, Jane Gard and Sally Fish, who promptly donated. Another neighbor, Jeanine Voix, and, of course, Sue, who is always there for me, also gave blood. I needed three pints, and five were waiting, which touched me so much that I cried.

While I was having the worst day of my life, one of the volunteer massage therapists came into my room and offered to give me a massage. I asked the therapist whether she knew the ingredients of the massage oil, explaining that I'm very allergic to lanolin. The container wasn't labeled, but she assured me that there was no lanolin in the oil.

The massage was very relaxing, and I was beginning to feel better. Then the hives began to appear. In fifteen minutes, they had spread over my body until I had full-body hives—from my face, including my eyelids, to my toes. I went from relaxed to out of my mind with itching. Craig rang for the nurse, but she couldn't do anything without doctor's orders. It took more than thirty minutes to get me a shot of Benedryl. Within an hour the hives subsided and I fell asleep wondering what else could possibly happen.

Later that afternoon I told Craig I wanted him to spend the night in the hospital. I said, "I'm really afraid I'm going to die tonight. Please don't leave me." But I didn't die. We both slept through the night fairly well except that I was up and down constantly going to the bathroom.

On Sunday, Dr. McAuliffe suggested that another oncologist, Bobbie Head, examine me. Dr. Head came in and said, "Get her off all of these antibiotics. This is not an infection. This is a chemo response and the antibiotics are making her worse."

They took me off the antibiotics, and I began to feel hopeful. I was very angry with all my doctors because I hadn't improved. My own oncologist, Dr. Spivack, had not called me, and I didn't know whether he had been in contact with Dr. Oppenheim or Dr. McAuliffe. I thought, "Doesn't anybody care?" (I later learned that Dr. Spivack *had* been in frequent contact with Dr. Oppenheim.)

On Monday everything reversed. They were able to isolate a bacterium that had caused an infection. The bacterium, Clostridium difficile, is very uncommon, and most doctors don't test for it. But it turned out that Dr. McAuliffe had ordered three different cultures for it because he'd had a hunch that's what it was. The first two cultures had been negative, but he persisted and was proven right on the third try.

The medication I needed was Vancomycin, which costs about $200 for a week's supply and is hard to find. I began to feel better within a couple of days after the drug was administered. But I was told not to get my hopes up too high because it takes a long time to get rid of this particular bug.

The days went by slowly, each day bringing terrible diarrhea, sometimes nausea. Each day, I feared I would never get out of the hospital. But Doctors Oppenheim and McAuliffe came to see me twice a day, and I felt that as long as they were seeing me and talking to me I was going to be okay. When I finally did get out of the hospital on July 31, I had an enormous emotional rush. I was really going home. I was really going to get well from this. I could go back and live more of my life. I hadn't realized until that moment how truly, truly scared I had been.

Looking back on this difficult time, I keep asking myself why it took so long to get the proper treatment. I blame myself for part of it. When I first became ill and during the following week when I was calling Dr. Spivack with daily reports, I communicated in the same businesslike tone of voice I would use to schedule an appointment. Now I realize I could have communicated more assertively, that I could have used a more demanding tone and said more clearly that I needed attention, that this was *not* an ordinary chemo reaction. Or I could have asked a friend or family member to call for me (indicating that I was too sick to call for myself) and say that I was extremely ill and needed treatment right away. It was a lesson learned: don't back down when you know you're sick. Tell the doctor in a way that he or she will hear you, even if you have to cry or raise your voice.

Dancing with the Doctors

I have become aware of the effect that medical people have on me: a word, a look, a voice inflection, the response to a question. I try to read between the lines: What is he saying? What isn't he saying? What does he really mean? And every time I go to the oncologist's, I want a report card. "Am I doing better? Am I doing worse?" I don't think he understands my need for that. Health care professionals should know that patients leave every appointment with hope or no hope, based on what they say—and don't say—with their body language.

A few months after my colon resection, which was the first surgery, to remove the original cancer tumor, Craig and I asked the oncologist, "What about further surgery, to remove the metastases?"

The answer was, "In Stage Four cancer, there's no evidence that another surgery would increase your life span." That's not what I wanted to hear. I wanted to hear, "Go for it."

Afterwards, Craig said, "The oncologist deals in chemotherapy—that's the product he knows; that's the product he sells. Let's get some more opinions."

We asked Dr. Spivack whether it would be worth going to see another oncologist, Dr. Alan Venook, who specializes in cancer metastasized to the liver. Dr. Spivack said, "Yes, it's always good to get more information. But I'm not sure you will be satisfied because he'll tell you what you don't want to hear, which is that right now you are not operable."

Craig said, "What we want to find out is what we have to do to get operable."

Dr. Spivack said, "Go."

So we went to see Dr. Venook. We wanted to know, "What now? If I can't have surgery, what else can we do?" His advice was to go off the 5FU, because it wasn't working. He said I could probably consider myself in a semiremission state, enjoy my life, and do one of three things: One, "Wait until you get a tumor, and then deal with it." Two, "We could put you on a different chemotherapy, Mitomicin-C, which is also used for colon cancer." Three, "You could go to the Southwest Oncology Group in San Antonio where they're testing some newer drugs, which we may have here at U.C. in three or four months."

We walked back across the street to Dr. Spivack and told him what Dr. Venook had said. Dr. Spivack said, "I totally disagree. The 5FU hasn't failed you yet. In fact, I'd like to put you on a continuous dose."

I said, "I'm lost. You're both scaring me."

He said, "I think you need a third opinion. I think you should go to the Mayo Clinic in Minnesota or Sloan-Kettering in New York or M.D. Anderson in Texas to get it."

About the same time, I also had to see Dr. McAuliffe because I had a hemorrhoid. He examined me and told me he thought the surgery had healed appropriately. He then spent extra time chatting with me, telling me stories about his patients. One had Stage Four colon cancer seven years ago and is still walking around, another took the same chemo I was taking and her cancer went into remission, and so on. He said, "This is anecdotal stuff. It's not based on research. I just want you to know that there's always hope. Don't give up, no matter what we say, because we doctors don't know everything." *That's* what I wanted to hear. I knew the statistics for my disease and I knew that he knew them, too.

I told Dr. McAuliffe what Dr. Venook and Dr. Spivack had said and asked him what I should do. He thought I should go to M.D. Anderson.

I said, "Couldn't I just package up my reports and send them off?"

He said, "They need to see you. Your records belie your presence. On the outside you are so strong and so healthy, you're psychologically sound, you're emotionally stable . . . they need to see that you're fighting this thing and doing a hell of a job." Once again Dr. McAuliffe had said the most positive, hopeful things anyone had said to me. He made me feel good. I appreciated the time he took to bolster my spirits. I actually felt physically better when I left his office.

I became aware that I had been nervous about even asking about other treatment options because I felt foolish having hope when there was so little to be had. I was afraid to ask, "What about this hyperthermia treatment, this oxygen treatment, this drug and that drug?" because I feared the response, "No, Linda . . . it's not going to work in your case . . . you're not going to make it." But I decided to stop feeling that way. What does it matter what doctors think of me? What does it matter if they think I'm a desperately hopeful person? I want them to think of me as the person in the one percent bracket who outlived the average.

In December 1992, my CT (Computed Tomography) scan showed that the tumors in my liver had shrunk so much that they were invisible except for one about the size of a nickel. There were no new tumors anywhere that they could find. My chest was still clear. Of course, the CT has trouble picking up flat cancer tumors and cells. But we had such great progress in the liver that Dr. Spivack assumed the other tumors also had either shrunk or gone away.

It was the best Christmas present, to find out that I was no longer in the "months only" category. It was the first time I'd been able to explore the idea of remission. But I found myself being fairly reserved about it. I said, "Craig, why can't I get excited?" He said, "It's sort of like jumping up and down inside a cave. Eventually you knock your head on something."

I asked Dr. Spivack to define "remission." He said, "It means that with our current technology, we can't find measurable evidence of cancer. The CT scan would be clear and the CEA would be down to zero."

"What would it mean if things stay the way they are—no further growth but still evidence of cancer cells?"

"That's considered partial remission."

By February my CEA had gone up to 60. That was not towards remission. It was going back the other way. I was angry and depressed. Earlier I had complained about nausea, loss of taste, and fatigue, so Dr. Spivack had lowered my chemotherapy doses. I thought that lowering the doses had contributed to the new growth. I said, "Look, I want you to increase my doses because my goal is not just to eliminate the nausea. I'll probably have that no matter what the dose. My goal is to increase the likelihood that I will live longer. I don't mind spending the next month being ill if it can add a year, or even a few months, to my life."

He said, "Okay. But we can't make you sick like you were in July and worry about you even living through a treatment."

In May 1993, I saw an oncologist at Stanford Medical Center, Dr. Sikic, for another opinion. As a result I decided not to go to Kettering or Mayo or M.D. Anderson. Dr. Sikic was able to help me understand the whys and why-nots of various treatments. After we talked to him, I felt more comfortable about making decisions. But I had to hear one more time how serious my condition was.

Dr. Sikic said that regardless of how well I was doing or how well I looked, the only thing they could go by is what they saw inside my body at the time of initial surgery. The inside is in much worse condition than the outside. No one can ever promise me more than months, he told me. I said, "Does that mean something could happen quickly that would turn things around?"

He said, "Exactly. You could have resistant cells, you could have fast-growing cells, you could develop a tumor that creates a blockage. Bingo."

I said, "What else could I die from?" I'd asked this of two or three doctors. Dr. Spivack had told me, "You'll probably die from liver malfunction." Dr. Venook had said, "You won't live long enough to die from the liver metastasis. You'll probably die from a kink or a blockage in your colon." Dr. Sikic told me, "You don't even want to know all the things you could die from—the cancer could metastasize to any area in your body, you could die from toxicity from your chemo, you could die because the Medivac helicopter crashes on your head on your way out of this hospital. Keep in mind that everything is unpredictable." He also said that some people live for years and years on chemo. On the one hand, that sounded really good . . . but on chemo every week? Getting sick and feeling crummy? I'm not so sure I want that.

Just talking about dying and the fact that I had a shorter life-span no matter how well I looked, about how unpredictable this disease is, made it really difficult. I had to go through all the acceptance stages all over again, and it took me a week to get over the depression. Still, I found it unbelievable. I thought, "Hah, they told me this last year and look at me now."

Dr. Samuel Spivack
(Linda's oncologist)

~~⊛~~

A doctor's time with patients should be focussed on how they're feeling, how they're eating, what they're experiencing when they're not in the doctor's office, what they're thinking about. Patients not only need to report their experiences, they need to editorialize on them. Not every patient can do that.

Linda was so intelligent and organized. She also had the skill of communicating. Some patients will slap a bottle of medicine down on the desk and say, "Your damn medicine didn't work." Linda's communication skills were so refined that we could talk about what worked and what didn't work without it threatening either of us.

A patient needs to have some way of communicating relevant facts to the doctor in a language he can understand efficiently. I have people keep a simple diary listing their symptoms. That gives me a broader view. I need to be able to incorporate these facts into my thought process in order to make a diagnostic or therapeutic evaluation.

I try to respect patients as people. The patient and the doctor have to be on an equal footing if they're going to have an equal exchange. That means taking extra time and directing attention to the patient, listening and responding to him or her. Sitting down instead of towering over the patient in a white coat while he or she is undressed. There's no dialogue that way. And if there can't be a dialogue, there can't be a successful doctor-patient relationship.

I'd say that 95 percent of my patients want as much information as they can get. Many are already in support groups and have a lot of information. In that sense, Linda wasn't unusual. But in her ability to integrate that information, she was certainly above the average. She was also computer literate, so she could get on-line with MedLine or the National Cancer Institute PDQ system. People who aren't that gifted can still get information through organizations like Planetree here in San Francisco.

Linda did better than the average patient, in part because for her the glass was half full, not half empty. If a patient is always complaining about the side effects of treatment, I'm unlikely to push the drugs as hard. It has to do, partly, with what's allowed or tolerated by the patient. A patient's psychological state affects longevity. At some point, the head really is connected to the body.

During one visit, I prevailed on Linda to allow two medical students to examine her. Afterward she told us, from the patient's point of view, what the doctor-patient relationship should be. It was a concise, sensitive explanation, about rapport, respect, and listening. I had wanted her to make a videotape I could show to my students. Now I hope her book will communicate some of those things she cared so deeply about.

It wasn't only Linda's spirit that kept her going. She had a loving husband who stood by her. She had a nice home. She was successful in her life—a fulfilled person. She was not angry or bitter. Sure, she was curtailed early in life, but she had enough accomplishments to look back on to feel that she had created something. And she had a child who needed her desperately. Those were reasons to go on living.

Taking the Cure

⚜

For every symptom, there's a medication. For every medication, there's a side effect. And for every side effect, there's another medication, and another side effect, and on, and on.

I started chemo treatments in June 1992, about two weeks after my initial surgery. I dreaded the days I had to go into San Francisco to Dr. Spivack's office for a chemo infusion. It took a half day of my time, and I only had a half day of energy. I could have been doing something more pleasant.

Going to an oncologist's office, sitting in a waiting room with other people who have cancer, reminded me I had it, too. First, there was the waiting. I would sit there, nervous, until they called me in. They would weigh me and take my blood pressure, and then this woman I call "Madame Dracula" would draw my blood. Then Dr. Spivack did a general checkup. Then he found a vein and started the IV for the chemo.

The wait was a horror that you can't imagine unless you've been a cancer patient. Most of the other people were older than I was, but some were younger. I would look at them and wonder, "Are you the patient or are you the friend, the husband, the mother? What kind of pain are you living with? How much time do you have?" All around me were people with white, pasty faces, nauseous from chemo or radiation; people wearing bandanas or wigs to cover their baldness; people with tears in their eyes; people with children curled up in their laps; people holding year-old magazines, but too preoccupied with cancer to notice.

In November, a surgeon inserted a "PasPort" under the skin on my arm so blood could be drawn or chemo given without having to poke into a vein each time. The "port" where the needle enters is connected to a tube that goes into my vein and is pulled through the vein into my chest. At first, I felt it under my arm every time I reached for something. I had to change my closet around because I couldn't reach for things on the top shelf. Later it wasn't noticeable.

The chemo had a lot of side effects. It made me very lethargic. Dragging myself out of bed became a big deal. I was nearly always nauseous, and the medication for the nausea increased the lethargy. I had almost constant diarrhea and I kept trying to pump myself full of liquids to keep from dehydrating.

The chemo affected my sense of taste. At Thanksgiving, I knew I was eating turkey and dressing from the smell, not from the taste. By December all my taste buds were gone except bitter. If I put a lot of salt or sugar on something, I could taste it. Then I got a sort of metallic taste in my mouth that I couldn't get rid of, so I started eating Altoids, those peppermint candies that are almost hot to the taste. The chemo also dries up the mucous membranes of the body, so my mouth and nose had sores in them, and I kept having nosebleeds.

In May 1993, Dr. Spivack put me on a continuous infusion. (My dad calls it "continuous confusion.") It's a device that pumps chemo into an IV tube inserted in the PasPort. The pump is about the size of a Sony Walkman and I wore it on a belt around my waist. The tube was long enough to tuck into my shirt and down my sleeve. It didn't show much, but I never forgot it was there. At night I put the pump on the floor next to the bed so I could roll around.

In July 1993, I started taking a time-released morphine, MS Contin, orally, 60 mg morning and night. I also took a liquid morphine when I had breakthrough pain that the MS Contin couldn't relieve. Some days I needed to take it a lot and some days I didn't need it at all. I also took a sedative called Ativan at night. Then, because the morphine is so constipating, I had to take stool softeners and laxatives, because one of the worst things that could happen to me would be to have a bowel impaction or some kind of rupture or perforation.

After I had been taking the morphine for a while, I stopped feeling the side effects. But at the beginning, I was disoriented. I was sleepy and sometimes I had trouble standing up. My blood pressure dropped. The first few days, I had some hallucinations. I don't remember them, but Craig says that one time I sat up in bed and I was doing things with my hands. I don't know if I had my eyes open or not. I told him I had been dreaming I was filling a mold with air molecules, and then I was going to be able to open the mold and it was going to be an animal shape made out of air molecules. It made perfect sense to me at the time.

Patient as Customer

❧

*Companies have studied the "walk-away" period—how long
customers will wait before they say, "The hell with you,"
and walk away. I'm probably willing to spend fifteen
minutes most places, but then I leave and say, "You call me."
But how can you walk away and go to a different hospital
when that's where your doctor wants you to go?*

Before my first surgery, I got a phone call from someone at California Pacific Medical Center in San Francisco saying that I had to have some blood tests done. I asked if I could have them done locally at Marin General. She said, "No, we want you to have them done here."

I said, "I have cancer and I don't feel like coming there. It's an hour to drive there, probably an hour to get the tests done, including the wait, and an hour back. All she said was, "We need to register you here, too. We're a very busy hospital."

The next day the hospital called again. A different person. She said, "I need to preregister you."

I said, "Someone called yesterday and told me I had to come into the hospital to register and get blood tests done."

She said, "Oh, no, I can preregister you over the phone, and you can have the blood tests done anywhere."

A few weeks later, I went to Marin General Hospital for a CT scan. The woman at the information desk said, "Have a seat and someone will call you in a minute."

I was walking slowly because I was hurting. Sue was with me and we sat down in chairs that must have been designed for Ichabod Crane, they were so hard and stiff. They forced you to sit straight up with your legs out in front of you, and they were permanently fixed to the floor so you couldn't move them. This was a waiting room unfit for a sick or disabled person, and yet this was the first place sick people had to go.

A woman with a walker came in behind me. She was told the same thing: "Go sit down and wait to be called." But there was no seat she could get to with her walker. We watched as she moved painfully across the room trying to find a place to sit down. And we thought, "Does anyone here care about the patients?"

Then, just as I had gotten myself halfway comfortable, I had to get up and walk over to a cubicle to be "processed." I thought they should come to you, with something like a manicurist's table they could roll over to your chair so you don't have to get up.

The woman didn't even look up at me as I entered her cubicle. She just stared at her computer and asked, "How are you?"

I said, "I have cancer, how are you?"

She said dryly, still without looking at me, "Sorry. Name?" Then she pulled my name up on the computer and asked for my insurance card.

I said, "I was just here a few days ago. I'm sure you have it in your records."

"We have to ask for it every time in case it's changed."

"Why can't you just ask me if it's changed?" I was getting feisty by now, since I was so frustrated by what seemed to be ridiculous procedures.

"Well, that's our policy." There it was, that word "policy." When will organizations learn to teach people to think instead of having them memorize policies?

When we finally got upstairs for the CT scan, Sue and I were laughing so hard that the other patients in the radiology waiting room must have thought we were terribly disrespectful. It seemed there was no end to the moronic things people do to other people who are supposed to be treated like customers.

In December, I checked into U.C. Medical Center at 12:15 for a CT scan that was finally done about 2:30. It was a miserable day. U.C. is like the slowest cafeteria line you've ever gone through: stop here, get this, go there, get that. At each place you wait.

First, they had me change into hospital pajamas and sit in the waiting room. Then I had to drink a disgusting liquid, two glasses of it. I gagged on every sip. I had to sit with a garbage can next to me in case I vomited. Then they took me into another room where I lay on a gurney while a nurse put an IV in my arm. He stuck me several times, trying to find the vein. I said, "I know you're not going to have any luck with that vein. It never cooperates."

"That's all right, it looks good." No luck.

"I suggest this other vein."

"Oh, we don't like to use that vein. We like to try to use the ones in the hands or in the forearm."

"Just use this vein, you'll be surprised."

"Let's try this one first."

After a few more tries, he used the one I had told him to use. To make things worse, he had body odor. Every time he came near me, I had to hold my breath.

Then I lay there waiting for a while, until somebody finally told me to go to the scanner room. I was delighted finally to be called to the scanner, but I was not comfortable getting there. This was not a private part of the hospital. There were lots of people in the hallway, and there I was wearing those silly hospital pajamas and carrying my own IV bag.

Finally, I lay down on the CT scanner table and the technicians put my hands over my head. Then they disappeared. God knows what they were doing. They didn't tell me. They just left me lying there with the IV stuck in my arm and my arms up over my head.

After a while they came back and adjusted the machine and slid me back and forth inside the "hole" part of what looked like a mechanical donut. Then somebody said, "Okay, we're going to start. We'll need to insert the enema tip now." I thought, "Hey! No one said anything about an enema tip! What's that got to do with a CT scan?" But I was too dumbstruck to ask. So I let them roll me over on my side and insert the tip, while they explained that they were filling my bowels with dye. Then they shamelessly said, "Roll over onto your back and be careful not to let the tip slide out."

Then they started the scanner. It took about forty-five minutes. I was in a very uncomfortable position, with all this stuff being pumped into my body, and being slid back and forth through the hole of a donut while alternately holding my breath and letting it go. Finally, the technician removed the fluid they had pumped into my rear end, took the IV out of my arm, and said in a cheery voice, "Okay, you're done." And I was exhausted.

They could make it easier. They could give you a sheet of paper describing the process you're about to go through and setting time expectations. When you wait in line at Disneyland, a sign tells you how long it will be from where you are to your ride. If it takes less time, you're happy. And why isn't there a private place where you can wait with your family, with simple access to the scanning rooms? I don't need for the rest of the world to know I'm sick.

When I had a barium enema at Marin General, the technician set a perfect example of how to communicate. Even though I was in a silly hospital nightgown, he treated me respectfully, explaining the procedure while we were both standing up. He said, "If you get uncomfortable in any way, let me know. The biggest fear people have is that this stuff will leak out of their bodies and make a big mess on the table. But that's no big deal. It happens. All we do is clean up and start over." He made it so comfortable for me to be a patient. He never treated me like an unfortunate cancer victim, but he also never treated me like a well person. It was as if he felt I was special and needed to be treated with care. He was very kind and very gentle.

Hospitals know how to make you comfortable, if they want to. One of the wonderful things about Marin General is an area called the Shared Care Unit. The nurses, doctors, patients, and families all share in the care of the patient—except that while I was there, the nurses were so fantastic that I had to do very little to care for myself. They did everything. They worried about me. They cared about me. They hugged me. They actually made me feel like they loved me!

Marin General also provides a lot of special volunteer services such as massage therapists and hair stylists. An art therapist came in with water color markers, paintbrushes, and water, and showed me how to paint. I learned it took a great deal less energy for me to sit and concentrate on painting than to talk or read or watch television. It was a wonderful feeling. I did two paintings while I was there, the first ever in my life; they were definitely refrigerator-door quality, if not better. I gave them to two of my favorite nurses, who treated them like masterpieces.

It was completely different when I was at U.C. Medical Center in March 1993. At U.C. the focus is clearly research and student training, not patient care.

The purpose of putting me in the hospital was to alleviate dehydration. But it was about five hours before they started treating me for it. And they didn't feed me properly for three days. They brought trays to my room, but not anything I could eat. I told the dietitian, "I can't eat dairy products unless you bring me Lactaid. I can't eat anything citrus or sour because I have sores inside my mouth, and broth is too salty and it's not enough. I need something with a little bit of bulk."

Three times a day my trays would come with two ice creams, a popsicle, orange juice, and a bowl of broth. I would starve between bowls of broth. I asked the dietitian, "Would you please bring a snack between the meals?" But the snacks would come at the same time as the meals, and they would be things I couldn't eat. Finally I called my friend Judy Hulka and said, "Judy, I'm starving, please bring me something!" She brought me yogurt, and Craig brought me Lactaid. Later I found out that U.C. has a great cafeteria. If I'd known, I'd have dragged my IV pole down there and gotten a tray.

I was very angry that I got no attention. The nurses never came into my room unless they were going to give me medicine or check vital signs. I decided I wanted to get out of there; I figured I would be better off at home. So I got out of bed and went into the hallway. Nobody was looking so I grabbed my chart out of the slot outside the door to find out what the doctor was saying about me. There were only a couple of pages, and I thought, "I wonder where my history is?" So I wandered down the hall to the nurses' station. None of the nurses even looked up. There was a carousel of binders with patients' medical histories in them. Mine was about two or three inches thick. I took it back to my room, and read the whole thing. It took about an hour.

Then I decided to work up my strength. I went into the hall and walked about twenty or thirty rotations around the floor. Then I left the floor. Nobody paid any attention. No one at the nurses' station looked up to see if I was okay. So I decided to speed up. I thought, "I'm going to go faster and faster." I'm not sure I was in my right mind. All I knew was that I wanted to be noticed. I took the binder with my history back to the nurses' station and put it in the wrong slot on purpose. I visualized that a doctor would come in and say, "Where's Mrs. Mukai's chart?" "Well, I don't know, I put it right there." "It's not there, someone must have done something with it!" "Who took it?" No one would ever know I was the one who took it.

Dr. Spivack came to see me once or twice every day. When I complained to him about the hospital's care, he suggested I write a letter to the hospital. He thought I had more power to be heard than he had. Think of it, a hospital that doesn't listen to its doctors' concerns about how their patients are treated. How could I possibly believe they would listen to me?

Hospital staff can drive you crazy. When I was in Marin General after the colostomy, I asked a nurse, "Is anybody comparing the tumor they just took out with the tumor they took out last year to see if there was any difference in the type of cell?" I wanted to know if the cell had mutated to a more resistant type, whether it was more resistant to the chemo, and whether that meant I should be changing chemos. I thought it was a fairly intelligent question.

So I picked up the phone in my hospital room and asked the operator, "May I please speak to the pathologist?"

She said, "Who are you?"

"A patient."

"We don't connect patients to pathologists."

"Why not?"

"Because you can't talk to them."

"Why not?"

"You have to go through your doctor."

"Why?"

"That's our policy." (That word again!)

I called the nurse: "Nurse, what is the phone extension of the pathology department?" "2113." "Thank you."

Beep-beep-beep-beep. "Hello, is this the pathologist?"

"Yes."

"This is Linda Mukai. I'm a patient in 2953 and I just had a colostomy. Would you please call and get the slides from my original tumor over at California Pacific Medical Center and compare the cell type with my current tumor so I know whether I have a different type of cell in this tumor?"

"Oh, sure, we'd be glad to!" Click.

I never heard from them again.

Janis

In December, another lesson: if I'm really going to be of help to Linda, I have to let go of old communication patterns, all that learned behavior that gets in the way. What happened was that Linda asked me to drive her to San Francisco for a doctor's appointment, a visit that would take a full afternoon. I wasn't busy. I could easily have said, "Yes," unconditionally; instead I said, "Yes, *but . . . but* I'll take you in and then come back and pick you up."

For her part, Linda could have said, "Great." Instead, she said, "Oh, no, that's too much trouble, I don't want you to waste the whole day."

I countered with, "No, no, that's fine, I'm glad to do it," and by then we were caught in an old pattern from which we couldn't seem to extricate ourselves. It was like picking up the check in a restaurant: "I'll take care of it." "No, no, it's my turn." "No, listen, I really want to." "No, no, I'm not going to let you. . . ." Silly stuff in a restaurant; not silly when one of you is fighting cancer.

As it turned out, Linda's mother—who never drives on freeways—drove her to the doctor, and they got there and back just fine. I felt angry at myself for not being willing to say an unconditional "yes" right away, and I also felt a little miffed at Linda for not accepting at face value my statement that I didn't mind taking her in and coming back. We both learned something important about communication that day.

The test results were good news. The CT scan showed no tumors in her abdomen, and fewer, smaller tumors in her liver. As usual, I refused to let myself feel absolutely happy and then I felt angry with myself for being negative. I couldn't let go of my fantasy scenario, where the angel comes down and says, "Sorry, you weren't on our list after all, we apologize for the inconvenience." I was impatient. I wanted to write the ending to this story: "And Linda lived happily ever after."

On Valentine's Day 1993, Linda was still alive. I was thankful she had made it that far—more than thankful, hopeful, even prayerful, that the sheer force of her will could overwhelm the bad guys that have attacked her body. "If anyone can force those bad guys out just by being willful," I thought, "it's Linda." She seemed to be drawing on an inner source of strength the depth of which I had barely even glimpsed.

Yet it was during those same months that I first began to believe Linda might actually die. Since we began this book, five people I knew have died. Two of them, my Aunt Dee and Uncle

Sid, were elderly and ill, the first of my parents' generation to go. Two of them, Beverly and Jay, were my peers. And one, Duncan, was so young that I experienced his death as a rift in time and can still hardly speak his name without feeling the rush of tears.

And now I have begun to accept the possibility that the disease could overwhelm Linda. I don't even want to write the words. Words are so powerful, I worry that speaking or writing them can make things happen. And yet . . . if there *is* such magic, there must also be magic that can make people well.

I have also begun to notice in myself a tendency to accept Linda's condition: "Linda is a sick person," I think. "Linda might only have a few months to live." I think we grow callouses and I am growing one around my feelings for Linda. It's like catching myself in a shrug: "That's the way it is. What can I do?" I feel ashamed of that shrug. I think I should feel pain every time I think about Linda's illness and I should think about it all the time. But I can't.

And so I learn another lesson: there are too many "shoulds." There's a set of shoulds for the person who has cancer, a set for that person's loved ones, and another for that person's close friends. There are "shoulds" for business colleagues and acquaintances and caregivers. Everyone wants to know exactly what to do and think and feel, as if that knowledge will make the whole thing easier. But there is no "right" way to feel or even to behave. Every person—patient, relative, friend, or caregiver—experiences a serious illness differently. Every person has different needs, and every person has something different to give.

What's important, as Linda helps me see and continues to help me understand, is learning to understand what I need and want, what frightens me, what I am capable of giving. To pay attention. To recognize that sometimes I won't know what to do or even what to feel. It would be nice to have a book of rules. But there isn't any such book; we have to make it up as we go. And a rule book wouldn't make it easy. It won't ever be easy.

FAMILY

Telling Our Son

*I don't know how much Matt understands. At least he
knows we haven't lied to him. We've tried to tell him the
facts as we know them, without robbing him of hope.*

One of my first thoughts was, "Matt is only seven years old. I don't
want Craig to raise him alone. I hate for Matt not to have a
mother. I don't want to miss his growing up."

Craig and I had wanted a child so badly. We spent several
years fighting my infertility problems and then we were fortunate
enough to adopt Matthew as an infant. The thought of not being
able to see him grow up is devastating. I have to tell myself,
"What's important is what happens right now. We have to make
memories that will last his lifetime."

When I was diagnosed I told Judy Hulka, who wanted to
help in some way, "See if you can find a book that will tell me
how to tell Matt." She found a book on how leaves, trees, birds
and people die, and it was useful. But we knew it wasn't going to
be our first approach.

We wanted to tell him as much as we could before school
started, and we didn't tell any of his friends' parents until we told
him. We were afraid the parents might talk to each other about it
while the kids were listening. Kids put two and two together so
easily. If somebody came up to Matt and said, "I hear your mom's

dying," we wanted him to be able to say, "No, she's not. Right now, she's taking medicine; she's trying to get better."

First, we told him that I had a tummy problem and was going to have surgery. I'd had a hysterectomy four years earlier and he'd seen me feeling sick, recuperating over three months, and then becoming well. I was going in for another tummy surgery, and then we'd talk to him some more. That was the plan: incremental storytelling.

When I got home from the hospital, we told him that I had some tumors and that the doctors weren't able to get them all. I was going to be sick for a while longer. We were going to spend a lot of time researching doctors and medicines to make sure that we had the right kind of treatment so I could get better. That was Chapter Two.

Chapter Three came when I had my first chemo. I told him I was going to take this funny medicine. I said, "Have I told you about this medicine I'm taking? It's really funny, because while you are taking it, you actually get sicker than you were before. I might have diarrhea, I might throw up, I might even lose some hair."

He said, "Well that's stupid! Do the doctors know that?"

I said, "Yeah, they do." Then I asked, "What should happen if I lose my hair? Should I wear a wig? Or should I wear a hat? Or should I just go bald?"

He said, "You should go bald."

"Do you think I'll look like Michael Jordan?"

"No, you're not brown enough."

Chapter Four came unexpectedly. One day he lost a tooth. We put it under his pillow, but he couldn't find it. He started crying. I said, "OK, draw a picture of your tooth and write a letter to tell the tooth fairy that you lost it." He started drawing a picture of a tooth but he erased it about ten times, crying because it didn't look right. All of a sudden he stopped crying and said, "Mom, there's no tooth fairy."

I said, "There isn't?"

He said, "No, it's you and Dad."

"Who told you that?"

"My friends." He pinched my cheek, and said, "Tell the truth." I said, "OK, it's true. It's Mom and Dad."

"There is no Santa Claus either, is there?"

"Do you really think that?"

He looked at me, deep in thought, and said, "I'm not really sure and I don't know if I want to know."

I said, "There *is* a Santa Claus who lives in our hearts."

He said, "You and Dad are Santa."

"Yeah, we are."

Then I asked, "Remember the carrot we left for the reindeer? And how chewed up it was on Christmas morning? Well, I'm the one who chewed it." We laughed and laughed about the fact that he had finally learned this.

The next night, I said, "You know, last night we talked a lot about the truth, and I want you to know that we will always tell you the truth, no matter what. If you want to know the truth, you can just say, 'I want to know the truth.'" Then I said, "I want to talk to you about the truth of my sickness. The truth is that this is really a serious sickness. This funny medicine I'm taking is my chance to live longer and feel better. You've heard of cancer, haven't you?"

He said, "I've heard of that. You get that if you smoke."

I said, "Yes, some people who smoke get cancer."

"But you never smoked, Mom. Oh, but you told me once that you took a puff of a cigar."

"Yes, but you don't get cancer from one puff. I don't know how I got cancer."

He asked, "Are you going to die?"

"Everybody dies. The question is *when*. I'm hoping to be around for a long time. I really want to be here for you as you grow up, but it is possible that the cancer could get worse. When we know more, we'll tell you. But right now we don't know."

Then he lay flat on his bed and put his hands across his chest and said, "Are you going to look like this?" He'd been to a funeral and knew what bodies look like in a casket, so he was trying to look like that.

I said, "Oh, I don't know. What do you want me to look like?" We laughed and pretended we were dead and played around with silly poses.

Then it got serious again. I told him that if I did die I still planned to be there for him. He could imagine me as a little angel sitting on his shoulder and anytime he wanted to talk to me he could talk to me. He said, "Will you talk back?" I think he was afraid I was going to be a ghost.

I said, "No, you won't be able to hear me, but if you think in your mind, you'll probably know what I would have said to you. And then there will be times when you don't want me to be sitting on your shoulder. You're going to want me to go away so you can do something you don't want me to know about. All you have to do is say, 'Mom, skedaddle.' And I will." I told him that when I was a little kid, my great grandmother had told me that my great grandfather hadn't died, only his "house" had died, and that he was still with us. Even until my adulthood, I worried about him hanging around watching me. Matt and I laughed, and then we made a list of some things he wouldn't want me to see him doing.

One day, I took Matt with me to a chemo appointment. He found it very interesting to watch the needles prick my arm. Dr. Spivack was very good about explaining what was going on and letting Matt be a part of it. I don't know whether Matt was scared. He didn't say anything, but he was attentive to everything that went on. I let him rip my bandage off on the way home. He liked to look at the bloodstain on the inside of the bandage and the little puncture holes and bruises on my arms. I was proud of him that day—he had to be very grown up.

Another time I asked him, "If you were telling another kid about what it's like for your mom to have cancer, what would you say?"

He said, "That it's very weird because she has to take medicine that makes her sick."

I said, "Do you worry when I'm feeling sick?"

"Yeah."

"What would you tell the kid about what *you* feel having a mom who has cancer?"

He said, "It's hard. I cuddle with her. I help her do stuff that she needs help with. Like cleaning my room and helping her make her bed."

"Sometimes you go to the doctor with me, right?"

"Yeah. We have to sit around for a long time."

"I really appreciate all the things you do for me," I told him. "You make me proud of you."

Then he said, "If you die, can I have your arm?"

"Why?"

"I would cuddle with it."

I told him he couldn't have my arm, that things like that weren't done, so he said, "Couldn't I just have a finger to hold?" I said, "You might have a toenail or a lock of hair, but that's all."

Craig and I try to remember that children tend to think they're supposed to feel however their parents feel. I told Matt, "Sometimes you're going to see Dad or me laughing, sometimes you're going to see us crying, sometimes you might see me angry. You are going to have your own feelings, and sometimes you may feel the same way we feel. But you don't have to feel the same way. It always helps if we can talk about how we feel, so let's try to do that." It's added to the intimacy of our relationship, even though I know he only understands what's happening on a very elementary level. We're still building a foundation of truth and trust.

After the first Christmas, Matt began having more difficulty at home and at school. He started fidgeting more, a few motor tics started up, and he started doing and saying things that indicated he was troubled by my illness.

One day he said a prayer for me at school, something like, "God bless my mommy and help her get well from cancer." That let the teacher know that my illness was on his mind, because he'd never spoken up for prayers before.

He told me about it on his own a few days later. He said, "I said a prayer for you at school the other day."

I said, "What did you say?"

He told me, and I said that was really nice and I think things like that help me a lot.

He said, "I know you want to see me grow up and I want to help you."

Craig and I try to keep in mind that children often think they have magical powers. We don't want Matt to think he caused my disease or that he can make me well. One day when he got particularly angry with me, he said, "I can't even get mad at you, Mom. That's not fair."

I asked what he was thinking about. He said, "If I get angry at you, you might die."

I explained that he couldn't cause me to die *or* to get well by thinking about it or hoping it. I said that just because I had cancer didn't mean we wouldn't get mad at each other any more. Things were back to normal after a few weeks.

In July 1993, when I learned that the tumor in my pelvis had grown, I told him about it right away because my mom was weeping on and off all day. I said I had to go to another doctor to talk about radiation. I explained that radiation causes some side effects and I wasn't sure I was going to have it done. I said that Daddy and I were going to be talking about it a lot for a while, and if we seemed worried, it was because we wanted to do the right thing. I told him that this tumor was very stubborn and didn't seem to want to go away and the chemo wasn't helping.

Soon after that, I spent a day in bed, in a lot of pain. Craig took Matt out to the driving range and the movies. When they came home, Matt came into my room and gave me a big hug and said, "You know, Mom, when you die I'm going to put fifteen roses on your grave."

I noticed he said "when" and not "if." I said, "Fifteen! How come fifteen?"

He said, "Because that's how old I'm going to be when you die." Maybe it was wishful thinking or a premonition, or maybe he thought that fifteen would be old enough for him to handle it.

Then he said, "And then every year I'm going to put an extra rose on your grave so you remember how old I am." It overwhelmed me that my son, at the age of eight, had already created a ritual so we could "remember" each other throughout the years.

One night at bedtime, Matt told Craig, "I don't really believe in God."

Craig said, "Oh, really?"

Matt said, "Yeah, I think it's sort of like Santa Claus."

Craig said, "You know, you can believe whatever you want to believe. Some people believe in God, some don't. As you get older, you may change your mind several times."

Then Matt said, "I do believe in heaven, though."

Craig said, "Really? Well, where is heaven?"

Matt said, "It's up above the clouds."

Craig asked, "What happens when airplanes go up there?"

Matt said, "The souls have to move out of the way really fast."

When Craig told me about this, I thought, "Wow, I'm going to be up there dodging 747s. Or riding on them. Or letting them go through me!"

As time passed and Matt experienced many ups and downs with us, he became very inquisitive about how long I was going to live. One day I had to sit down and talk to him about his anger—I could tell that his little body was full of anger. I asked if he was mad at me for being sick and he admitted that he was. He wanted to know whose fault it was. I told him it wasn't anybody's fault. He asked, "How much longer are you going to live?" Over a week, he must have asked that question seventy-five different ways: "How long are you going to live? How old will you be when you die? How old will I be when you die? How many more years are you going to be alive?"

I finally said, "You know, when we found out that I had cancer, one of the first things we did was call your doctor and my doctor and our minister and ask them how much we should tell you. They all said to tell you the truth, and if there was something we didn't know, to say we didn't know, not to make up anything. That's what we've been doing. When we don't know something, we don't try to guess or make it up. It's hard to not know, but what we're trying to do is tell you the truth." He seemed to be more satisfied with that.

He asked, "What about Dr. Jang? How long is he going to live?" Our friend Chris Jang, who's in his thirties, also has colon cancer.

I said, "They caught his a little earlier, so he's in remission now, and he's doing better than I am."

Matt said, "It seems to me like God has been paying a little bit too much attention to Chris and not enough to you." All of a sudden, he believed in God again!

I asked Matt, "Why is it so important for you to know *when* I'm going to die?"

"Because that way I can stop thinking about it."

"But if we knew, do you really think we'd stop thinking about it? Wouldn't we just think, 'Six more months,' or 'Twelve more days'?"

"Yeah, but at least we would know!"

I said, "Sometimes I wish I knew, too, Matt, but not knowing gives me the freedom to hope. If I knew, I might give up trying. You wouldn't want that, would you?"

"No," he said, "but at least I wouldn't think about it every day."

"Instead of thinking about it every day, can you just be glad we had the day?"

"I'll try, Mom, but it's hard."

We hugged each other and I cried. He got me a tissue and we hugged some more.

Matt has obviously spent time thinking about my death. It pleases me that he's at a level of acceptance that he can say "when" now, although I know he will still have to go through the grieving stages when I die. I think he will be all right. He's a very smart boy, independent, sensitive, creative, and in some ways, very mature.

The Man I Love

Craig has been a gift from God. If anybody questions me about whether there's a God—it's a question that comes up a lot, as in: "My God, if there's a God why did he do this to you?"—I say, "Look at that man over there. There is somebody who had to be developed by somebody close to God."

One night Craig walked out of the shower nude and I had this enormous desire to drag him into bed and make love with him. I thought, "Oh, my gosh—how many more opportunities will we have to make love?"

Sex and cancer don't mix. There are too many things in the way: fatigue, medications, pain, self-consciousness. The drugs not only affect the libido, they also dry everything up. If we're going to have sex, we have to have all the products ready. But I have to do so many other things to my body every day—take medicines on time, take care of my stoma, change the dressing on my stent—that one of the last things I want to think about is using vaginal lubrication.

But I do have these thoughts every now and then: "Craig, · we've got to have sex, we may never get to do it again!" But it's scary for me and scary for Craig; he's afraid he's going to hurt me, and so when we do make love, it's very carefully, gingerly, which is not nearly as much fun.

During the first year, I felt guilty that I didn't initiate sex or even show much interest. Craig is a wonderful lover, and I'm sure he misses having a normal sex life. But he would never do anything to hurt me so he tells me not to worry, that we love each other and being together is all that matters right now.

For us, sex has become intimacy. It has become less of an act of intercourse than an act of closeness and sharing and caring. The actual going through the motions of having sex is no longer important. What's important is to snuggle up and be close to each other and talk. I think the talking and the holding is now our way of communicating our love and there's nothing better than that. It's been wonderful.

I think love transcends whatever difficulties there are. We have such a thing for each other that we're so glad to be together every night, every day that we have. That's really special. I think we've always had an incredible friendship. I can't imagine a marriage that was based totally on a sexual attraction. Thank God ours wasn't, because now we still have that depth of friendship and caring and loving. We're very fortunate to be attracted to each other, too, but there is so much more than that in our relationship.

One day I asked Craig how he was doing. He said, "I'm doing fine, you know, going day to day."

I said, "Honey, this doesn't help me at all. Knock off the macho business and tell me what's really going on. Please tell me how you're feeling."

He was able to do that. He was able to say, "I'm upset. I worry about you and I think about you every minute of the day. I feel helpless because I can't find a cure for you."

This man is so great. He is weathering this storm with me and he is really letting himself go through it. He cries. He laughs. He gets angry. He tries to be strong. He puts up this little shield. Then he peels it off so I can see what's underneath.

I came into the bedroom one night and he was sitting on the bed, big tears coming down, sobbing away. I put my arms around him and asked, "What's the matter?"

He said, "I really thought we had found each other in this world and were so lucky that nothing would ever come between us. We have been together almost fifteen years, and the longest we've been apart has been five days at a time. And even then, I can think of fewer than a handful of days where we didn't call each other. We have touched each other, talked to one another, almost every single day since June 12, 1979. How do I face endless days without you? How do I go from one to the other?" Then he wrote me a poem, a beautiful little poem called "Forever and a Day." He's seeking words to describe what he's going through.

I don't think too much about whether or not Craig will get married again after I'm gone, or whether he'll bring other women into my bedroom. It's not worth thinking about. I know that whatever he does will be done with a great deal of good judgment, and I trust him not to do anything that would make me feel bad if I happened to be hanging around looking over his shoulder. He feels strongly that he will never marry again. He might change his mind, but he seems convinced that the only reason for him to get married again would be to have children, and he says he doesn't want any more children. He says he can't imagine not being in this house after all we've done to make it such a nice place to live, and he wouldn't want to go through that process again. He feels at home here and likes having Matt here. It's the right place for him, at least for now.

It doesn't matter to me. I'd like to think that he will keep important things that we've purchased together, artwork and some single pieces of furniture that have sentimental value, that he won't give them up because the memories are too difficult. I find this speculation interesting, but I don't have any stake in it. After all, I can't take things with me.

Craig

*Family hugs and cancer have to go
hand in hand in order to survive.*

My first reaction was, "How the hell can this happen to my wife? She's too good to have something bad happen to her." At the same time I thought, "I don't want to have to do everything by myself. I don't want to have to raise our son alone." There was so much we had expected to do. It wasn't in the plans to have Matt and me go through it alone. You don't think of death and dying in your forties.

When Linda had her surgery and they couldn't get it all . . . I kept saying that day was the worst day of my life. But in actuality, the worst day of my life is still coming up.

All the cliche stuff about living each day like it's your last is now no longer a cliche. I still get upset with Linda if she leaves a cabinet door open and I walk into it. She still gets upset with me if I'm too tough on the boy. I think what she needs is for me to be me, the same person she married, the same person she's depended on for the last fifteen years. I think what I can give is mostly emotional support because she's amazingly tough. If the roles were reversed, I'd probably be slamming doors, punching holes in my house, because I couldn't understand, "Why me?" But she's amazingly resilient and amazingly strong. She's given all of us this sense of hope and good feeling and courage, which makes it easier for me.

We got married on December 22, 1979. I was thirty-two. I asked her to marry me thirty days after I met her. I was married the first time at age twenty-one to my childhood sweetheart, and I was divorced by age twenty-four. For eight years, I had a ball being single. Then Linda walked into my life and she was everything I wanted.

Before Linda and I did anything major, like purchasing our house, we asked, "What's the worst thing that could happen to us?" Right now that's what I'm doing: "If Linda is going to be gone, what is the worst thing that can happen to me and my family?" If I can prepare from a mental point of view, a financial point of view, and a parental point of view, then I think I can handle it.

To get ready, I have to figure out basic stuff. How I'm going to get Matt to school, how I'm going to be home when he gets home so he doesn't end up being a latchkey kid. Kids are so much more aware than we were. The worst thing we could do when we were kids was smoke in the bathroom. These kids might sit on the can and shoot up instead. So I think, "Can I work fewer days? Can I work early in the morning and get back at three o'clock in the afternoon? Or do I hire someone to pick him up from school and stay with him until I get home?"

Matt knows Mommy has cancer. I know he thinks about it. He asked, "Daddy, is Mommy going to have cancer all her life?" I said, "Yes, I think Mommy is always going to have cancer." I left the tag off, that cancer is going to kill Mommy.

I don't dare think of miracles. If you base your preparation on the miracle, and the miracle doesn't happen, you're left hanging in midair. I think what I've done is decide that I can raise Matt by myself. There are a lot of single parents who have proved it can be done. So if she's on her deathbed saying, "I'm sorry I can't be here with you 'til the end," I can tell her it's okay.

It's hardest when I think about the things we wanted to do. Linda and I have worked hard. I wanted to get to a place where we could do whatever we wanted. I think, "We're being cheated. It's not fair. If there is a God, then why is He doing this, in this way, at this time?"

Whatever comes up you deal with it at that time. I think it's a little ridiculous to try and handle this thing in an organized way. I told Linda I thought I should write a book called, "She's Okay, I'm Okay." If she's okay, I can stay positive. If she's not okay, I have to rely on defense mechanisms, such as, "Let's see if we can concentrate on helping her." Sometimes you fall back on memories of comfortable feelings and comfortable times, when things weren't so stressed out.

I was a longshoreman in college, and I used to work down in the holds of ships. You'd be on deck and then you'd go seventy or eighty feet down to the bottom, and then you'd climb back up to the deck. Having cancer in our lives is a lot like being on a ship that's continually moving around the world while you keep going down into the hold and back up again. Every time you pop up on deck, you're in a different place, with a different view. Each time you poke your head out of a porthole, you see something you hadn't seen before.

We have become closer. Our relationship is more intense because we don't know if we have next month or next year. If something is bothering us, we talk about it right then. We don't have time to play games.

We were talking about Magic Johnson having AIDS and that he has a life expectancy of about eight years and is starting to die. Matt said, "That's really too bad, he has a baby and he's married." Later, he was sassing Linda, and I got upset with him. I cornered him and started hammering on the table. I felt frustrated that anybody, whether he's eight or eighty years old, was not respecting another person who was in a life-threatening situation. I was frustrated that he was rude, was all the things I did not want to see in my boy. I remember hammering on the table and shouting, "You don't understand, you don't understand. You think Magic Johnson's feeling bad? Your mom is facing much more of a crisis than Magic Johnson." It was heavy for an eight-year-old. I started crying, still hammering on the table, and he started to cry. And Linda came up behind me, and she started crying and I thought, "Well, I'll just cry, let it out." Then we got in a family hug. A family hug can help you through another day.

Now Matt understands what's going on, but he's also afraid of it. One day when I was sick with a cold, he said, "Daddy, do you have cancer?" You don't think about cancer being contagious, but kids do. He might think he could get it the way he gets flus and colds. We're always after kids to wash their hands, wash the cups, not to lick off the same spoon as another kid. So a parent who has cancer will dish up something for a kid and the kid will say, "I'm not that hungry," because he's afraid there might be something on the food. You have to watch for some things you don't even really think about.

What has changed is that now we no longer want to waste time. All the things that we think, "I wonder if we should do this?" we just do it. If you can afford to do it and you have the time to do it, you might as well do it because you don't know if you're going to get another chance. If Linda gets really sick again, all the time or all the money in the world . . . even if I'd won the lotto . . . there's nothing we could do.

What hasn't changed is the love connection between Linda and me. We still love each other the most. We're always saying, "I love you the most," "No, I love you the most." That hasn't ever changed.

My Father

⟨◈⟩

I've grown closer to my dad. I find myself wanting to talk to him more and more. Since I've been an adult, my dad and I have been more like friends. But now it's become more a father-daughter relationship. He understands what I'm going through. I can tell him the worst of it without fear. He "fathers" me and I love it.

About a month after my diagnosis, we found out that my dad has colon cancer, too. It was shocking. Here he was, just sixty-eight years old. And here I was, forty-six. Both growing tumors at the same time. Dad had been to his doctor several times complaining about chest pains. After my diagnosis, he went back to his doctor, who finally determined that he had cancer.

When Craig and I went to Tucson that summer to see Dad and Bobbie, my stepmother, I wanted to make sure that I got some conversation time with Dad, to compare notes on our diseases. I realized that we had been saying we had the "same thing," but actually I have my colon cancer and he has his, and they're very different. What isn't different is that we love each other and we are grieving over each other's illness. We understand what the other is going through and it hurts terribly to know that we are sharing a miserable, painful disease.

The progression of our diseases has been somewhat different. A year after our initial surgeries, I was getting worse, but it seemed as if he was getting better. He'd had wonderful results from his exams. His CT scans were completely clear, although his CEA count was still abnormal so his doctors weren't sure what was going on. But he couldn't get himself to celebrate because I wasn't in the same position. I think he also knew that his situation could turn around very swiftly like mine did. But if I had my wish, he would celebrate these small wins. We get so few of them.

By November 1993, he was where I had been nearly a year before when there was very little showing up on the CT scan, but the CEA was still rising. They put him on more intensive chemo. He went in for a treatment every day for a week, then he got a week off.

At the same time, I told him I was feeling more and more sick and that I was starting to think about death. Because he hadn't seen me for a while, it was very hard for him to accept the fact that I was worse and probably wasn't going to get better. What used to be close communication broke down. He didn't want to talk about my declining treatment, my concerns about death. He tried to pump me up, to give me more hope, but I wanted to talk more honestly and I needed his understanding. I hoped we could get that closeness back.

In February 1994, he and Bobbie came here for five days. Neither of us felt very well, but we enjoyed being together. He told me that his chemo was failing him, so he was going to a cancer research facility in San Antonio to try an experimental drug. He would have to stay in San Antonio for some period of time.

Just as with other friends and family, I've learned to communicate with my dad in new ways. We push ourselves to be honest with each other about what's going on, about our feelings. There's no time left for holding back. But our relationship is based on more than our cancers. After one weekend we spent together last year, Dad and I had joyfully congratulated ourselves for not bringing up the "C" word once the entire time—we had had a great time together instead.

Jim
(Linda's father)

I felt this pain in my chest on my right side. It had nothing to do with cancer, just a pain in my ribs from some muscles that I hadn't been using. The doctor asked a lot of questions and found that I had been passing blood in my stools. Then I told him about Linda, and he said, "Whoa, that's something to check." The first lower G.I. (gastrointestinal exam) was all it took.

The worst of it was that Linda had it. I was hoping my prayers had been answered: "Give me the burden, take it from her, give it to me." To think that Linda's life might be shortened just kills me. I've always been an emotional slob. When the new Buicks come out I get all torn up. Made in America really turns me on.

The cancer itself isn't so bad as the physical reaction to it. The treatment is bad. It's annoying more than anything. It's a bad taste in your mouth, it's losing hair, it's a constancy of stomach disorder. You're not fit to do those things that you need to do. I get out of the car like an old man, a decrepit old fellow who has a heck of a time moving. I don't walk as fast as I used to. I don't walk as straight as I used to. I take somebody's arm. Sometimes I feel ugly and dirty. I feel like I smell.

From the beginning there's a thin line between treatment and torture. You never get through taking chemotherapy. You get a hiatus, then you take six weeks of chemo, maybe have two or three weeks off, then you go right back to it. The realization that you're going to put up with this for the rest of your life is demoralizing.

And the waiting in doctors' offices, the lying there for hours while the stuff is piped into my veins, the weakness from the aftereffects is boring and tedious. I truly believe more people die from the boredom cancer produces than from the cancer itself.

Linda and I have so many friends. I've got stacks of cards and prayers, all kinds of little gifts. I've got a baseball cap signed by Spanky McFarland of "The Little Rascals," and baseballs, and a little TV set and all these things that people seem to want to hoist on you to make you feel better. The thought makes you feel better. Someone going to the trouble of doing something for you to let you know that they're thinking about you or you're in their prayers.

Some people don't know how to react. They say, "Get well quick." That's ridiculous. You get cards and they all say, "Get well quick." I know their intentions are good, but they're kind of silly, aren't they?

I have been painting, drawing all my life. Occasionally one piece turns out nice and it's so satisfying. I always enjoyed my work. I get lost in it. That piece of paper in front of me is the most important thing in the world. I can sit there for hours.

One of the problems is you can't get cancer out of your mind. It's the first thing you think of in the morning when you wake. It's the last thing on your mind when you go to sleep at night. You wake up in the middle of the night and you say to yourself, "I've got cancer." In the morning the first thing you think of is, "I've got to go to the bathroom because I have cancer." It's just there. It's an incredible old being.

Linda laughed a lot the first few weeks. But I haven't heard any funny stories from her for a while. Doesn't seem so funny any more. It's the prolonging of the thing, it just goes on and on.

Sometimes you talk to your body and say, "Get away from me. I don't need you. You're trying to kill me." I want to gather up all the little bad cells, put them in a baggie, zip it up and drop it off the side of the world. Everybody sends you tapes and books about conquering your own fears and positive thinking and all this stuff. Pretty soon you say, "I'm sick of this stuff." I've had enough of sitting on vortexes and carrying lucky charms and things like that. People kept giving me things that are supposed to be lucky or psychic in some way. But I haven't researched all that because I haven't really had any strong need to believe in it. I'm sort of skeptical of it, not of the power of the mind, because I believe in that. I think I'm skeptical of the types who are represented by it.

I never got mad. I did deny it. I said, "Why me, of all people?" I always said that this is my world, the rest of you people are props. But this is reality. "Hey, wake up, dummy. This is part of your world whether you like it or not." I guess that's one of the mysteries of life. How we are going to die. I've dreamed since I was a little kid that I'd die in September of somebody cutting my throat. Sixty-nine Septembers have gone by, but no one's cut my throat. But I worried when they stuck a big needle in my jugular vein. They had a terrible time finding a place to put it in. I said, "It shouldn't surprise you guys if I take you off my Christmas list."

All of a sudden things become interesting that weren't interesting before. Those trees out there take on a beauty that they didn't to the extent they do now. When I was in the hospital, when I was finally able to get up and go to the bathroom by myself and I washed my hands, the water was fantastic. The feel of that cold clear matter. It wasn't water anymore, it was a blessing. To bathe is just beautiful. To see, to hear children, blooms of flowers, it sounds ridiculous but all of a sudden those things are all intensified in beauty. Those things that used to be important, like bills, I don't give a damn about bills, new cars, big deal.

You have to learn to accept people wanting to do things for you. You have to accept people's pity. The way they look at you sometimes. You can just see it in their face: "If it can happen to you, it can happen to me."

Sometimes I talk to my cancer, saying things like, "Dammit, what are you doing in there? Are you trying to kill me? Get away from me, you #%$&*%@!" But other than an occasional "damn," I rarely curse anymore, and I never really get mad these days. What good does it do? When the terrible droughts hit the Indian reservation in Northern Arizona, the Navajos don't pray for rain as most people would, they perform a special ceremony as a supplication to give them the strength to be content with the inevitable. Well, it's very difficult to be content with our lot, Linda's and mine. I still pray for a miracle to make us well, but we must content ourselves with the knowledge that there's no such thing as "Yawl get well quick now, you hear!"

When Linda called to tell me she had cancer, she asked me to make her a statue. I wanted to go to her, to see her, to hold her; I didn't want to be making a statue. But I made the statue. It took me a month. During that month I came down with the same cancer she had.

I called Linda's bronze statue Esperanza, which is Spanish for Hope. I believe in the power of Hope. I told Linda that Hope is limitless, especially when it is strengthened by prayer.

July 28, 1994

My sweet darling Linda,

At the bottom of page 274 in Tony Hillerman's book, *Sacred Clowns*, Navajo tribal officer Jim Chee is attempting to explain to his friend the "Navajo Way":

> This business of *hozho* . . . I'll use an example. Terrible drought, crops dead, sheep dying. Spring dried out. The Hopi, or the Christian . . . they pray for rain. The Navajo has the proper ceremony done to restore himself [herself] to harmony with the drought. You see what I mean. The system is designed to

recognize what's beyond human power to change, and then to change the human's attitude to be content with the inevitable. ["Herself" is my doing.]

Perhaps we of the "cancer clan" can learn from the Navajos. This could be a way to pacify our questions of, "Why me, God?" and "Why didn't the doctor catch it sooner?" and "What did I do wrong?"

But it isn't to say we should totally accept our lot and stop praying for a cure and lose hope of being healed. Perhaps the answer is that while there is a need to endure our illness with the proper attitude, in the Navajo Way, we must continue to pray and hope, for with prayer, hope is limitless.

Hurry and finish your book. I love it, and you, too, and the whole family.

Love, Papa

My Mother

I worry about my mother. I worry about her worrying about me.

I've never been more sure of anything than the fact my mother loves me. She has always shown me her love in many ways. When I was a child, she took me everywhere, held me up for others to see, told stories about how cute or smart she thought I was.

In my youth, I could hear her talking on the telephone telling her friends about the things I was doing. She had a way of talking about me that never sounded like bragging, but there was no doubt she loved me.

As a child, and even during my teen years and beyond, Mom and I were incredibly close. I don't remember ever raising my voice to her. I never wanted to hurt or disappoint her.

Some years ago she paid me the most incredible compliment. She and I were in a restaurant talking and I told her I admired the way she lived her life and that I was open to any advice she had for me. She thought for a moment and then she said, "There's no advice I would give you. You have a wonderful family and a successful career. You've succeeded, you're happy—what else is there?" To hear such words from my mother was like receiving the highest honors.

I remember Mom as nearly always sick when I was a kid. She has lupus and heart disease. The doctors prepared us to lose her when she was in her forties, but now she's in her seventies, looking better than ever. She had her first heart attack when I was in my teens, and I began then to be afraid that she would die . . . that I would lose her. In those days, Dad wasn't very attentive and my stepdad, Andy, was irascible and critical. I was a little afraid of him. I didn't think either Andy or my dad would want me if she died, and I didn't think I wanted them, either. I began to try to take care of her so she wouldn't get sick. I think Mom was relieved to know that I would always be there for her.

I had always heard about Mom's aches and pains; her illnesses were too serious to ignore. As an adult, I was mindful that I needed to be on guard at all times. When I went on a trip, I always let Mom know where I would be staying, just in case she needed me.

I felt guilty about living so far away—I couldn't be there for her every time she had a lupus attack. I wanted to take care of her as much as I could. I was concerned that Andy didn't visit her much in the hospital or that he might neglect her when she was at home.

When I got sick, my mom stood out as the most difficult person to tell about my diagnosis. I knew she would be devastated. And she was.

I called her and she was here the next day. When I had my initial surgery, she stayed overnight in my room at the hospital; she didn't trust the nurses to take proper care of me. She tries to hold her tears and concerns back so I won't worry, but I know her well enough to know she is extremely frightened. She keeps saying, "I wish I could trade places with you," or "It's just not fair," or

"It's just not the right order of things," or "What's going to happen to me?"

My mom and Craig's mom, March, take turns being here for us. When I was feeling well, no one needed to be here, but when I got worse, we had to have someone here all the time. "The Moms," as we call them, fix meals, shop, wait on me hand and foot. They take care of Matt and keep the household running. They are glad to be here and never complain, except to point out my housekeeper's errors. But I know they tire from so much stress and extra work. I love them more and more every day, and I feel guilty about letting them do so much.

After several months of my mother taking care of me, a strange thing happened. I started becoming angry with her. I thought she wasn't being nurturing. Later, it turned out that she thought I didn't want nurturing, but unfortunately it took a lot of emotional upheaval to determine the cause of our (my) problem.

I wanted Mom's attention in different ways than she was providing. I wanted her to listen to me because I had a lot of feelings I wanted to talk about and there weren't many people I could talk openly with. I wanted her to be there saying, "Oh, honey, honey, honey," patting me, holding me, saying, "There, there, there." I wanted her to play the mother role. I felt instead that she still needed me to "mommy" her, because she was in such pain over my illness.

One morning when she was leaving to go home and rest for a while, I tried to talk to her about how I was feeling. I went in and lay down on her bed with her. I said, "I'll miss you, but I'm glad you're going to get some rest." She patted me and said, "I'm not sure I should leave this soon." I said, "I'm going to be all right and you're going to be all right." She said, "I worry about you when I'm not with you. You're my daughter. I love you, I care about you and you've been the most important thing in my life." How could I broach a negative subject at a time like that?

I said, "Mom, I still need a mom." She said, "And I still need a daughter." I loved being needed by her, but I wanted her to hear how much I wanted and needed *her* right now.

After she left and I'd had time to compose my thoughts, I wrote her a letter. I didn't want to hurt her, but I wanted to get my point across. I said, "Here's what I need and here's what I don't need." I tried to make clear to her what my needs were in a way that wouldn't be terribly upsetting to her, although the letter wasn't as loving as I wanted it to be.

After she received the letter, she called, and we talked and talked. She said, "I missed all the clues. You've always been so strong, and so stoic, I thought you wanted your privacy. I left you alone because I thought that's what you wanted." She said she had felt unsure about how to comfort me. She saw me as so much in control, so strong and independent, that she couldn't see how to help me.

She was right. I often put on a strong front. She felt so bad about misreading my needs that I forgave her at once. She said all the right things. But I couldn't let it go. I found myself continuing to criticize her even after she said she was sorry. I had been saving up stuff for years, and I finally poured it all out. I ranted and raved at her over the phone for about an hour, and I threw in some real old baggage. That night I felt terrible about it. I didn't want to call her back because I didn't want to wake her up, but I wrote a note that said, "If I should die before tomorrow, please tell Mom that I didn't mean even one thing I said over the phone and that I'm sorry."

I called her the next day and said, "Mom, I want you to know that I apologize. It wasn't fair for me to bring up issues from earlier in my lifetime." She said, "Oh, no, that was okay." And I said, "No, it wasn't, Mom."

After we talked, I realized that if earlier I had taken the time to ask her, "What scares you the most about my illness, about what's going to happen," none of this would have ever taken place. I would have learned that one of her major concerns was becoming one of those old folks in a nursing home, abused by the staff with no one to check up on her.

I assured Mom that Craig would always be there for her, that he would never let anything bad happen to her, that she had nothing to worry about. She wasn't surprised, she said, because she knew that Craig is a man of strength, of character, and love, but she was worried that he would take a new direction in his life and that she might be forgotten.

Once Mom understood what I wanted from her was exactly what she wanted to give, she was delighted. And she's there for me now—she holds me when I cry, she strokes my head, she rubs my back, she says all the right things, and she means them. I got my mom back.

∽

June 30, 1993

Dear Mom,

I know we don't ordinarily write letters, but I wanted to say some things to you while you were here, and I kept failing miserably at it.

First of all, I want you to know that I've always loved you and needed you. You've always been there cheering me on, relating your pride in me, and listening to my day-to-day goings on. I've always been proud of you too. Of all the moms I knew, I always knew mine was the best.

When I was in my teens and you began to have failing health, it scared me to death. I was so afraid of losing you, for two reasons: (1) I loved you so much and (2) I didn't know what would happen to me (neither Andy nor Dad seemed interested enough to be there for me). Plus, as you know, Andy blamed me for your illness ("If you'd helped your mother more, this never would have happened").

It was then that I started trying to protect you from ever being sick again. I became careful of everything I said or did because I didn't want to upset you and cause you another heart attack.

Every time you would even hint that something was wrong or that you wanted something, I wanted to and tried to fix it for you or get it for you. I still enjoy doing things for you and buying things for you. You sacrificed a lot for me while I was growing up and I've wanted to make it up to you.

We've always stayed close and in touch; I've always wanted you to know how and what I'm doing and I've wanted to know how and what you're doing.

Now that I have cancer, the tables have turned somewhat. And this is where I have a hard time communicating with you. I want you to understand some things, but I don't want to upset you.

I think one thing that has happened is that now you are faced with the fears I had when we thought you were going to die early. I know you love me and don't want to lose me and I know you fear what is going to happen to you when I'm gone.

I also know you are careful about what you say to me because you don't want to upset me and make me feel worse.

These are the areas I need to address with you in this letter: (1) your fear of what will happen to you and (2) the way we talk to each other.

First of all, I know it must be scary to think about losing your daughter, your closest relative, the person you most count on for help and for love. This must be devastating. There is nothing I can do or say to reassure you that "everything will be all right." All I can point to is that you are a survivor. You have survived a difficult childhood, difficult marriages, and a lifetime of health problems. When Andy died, you were able to pick yourself up and get on with your life, and I think you have enjoyed this part of your life a great deal. Buying your own car and learning to rearrange your goals and priorities within a limited income was a challenge for you and you've accomplished it. But, of course, I've been here to help and you've counted on me for that. Now, this rug is being pulled out, and you are worried about your future.

It is probably little consolation for you to be told that Craig will always be here for you because you fear that nothing is certain. Although Craig loves you and will help you if you need it, he is not me and it will be different. His life will also go on and we don't know what the future holds for him.

So I guess what I'm trying to say is that you *will* survive. You may need to change your expectations ("Linda will always be here for me"), but you will have what you've always had—your own strong will, your friends, your intelligence, and your survival skills. Add Craig to that and your ability to cope will carry you through.

One thing I need from you is for you to remember that I'm helpless to do anything about the issue of "this is the wrong order of things." When you say that, it makes me feel as if I have failed you, and it sometimes seems that you are more concerned about your future than mine. I know this is *not* true, but please don't say that any more, at least not to me.

The second issue is regarding the way we talk to each other. As you know, I've been very sensitive to the things other people have said to me in response to learning that I have cancer.

At first, you and I were able to be very open about talking about my illness, but now it seems more difficult. I sense that you are afraid to talk to me about how I feel. Maybe you are trying not to upset me. Instead of asking me, you ask others how they think I'm doing. Maybe that is because I've been so stoic and appear to be so strong.

The truth is I'm very upset. I'm in pain a lot, sick a lot, get bad news a lot, fear the future of my illness, and I'm grieving over what and who I will be leaving behind. I need to be able to talk openly about this, and yet I hate to burden others with having to hear it over and over again. There are only a few people with whom I've been able to share my feelings openly: Craig, Diana, and a few others.

I'd like to be able to share more with you, but it's getting harder to do so. Sometimes it seems as if you are not listening or don't really want to hear about my illness. Sometimes—I don't know if you realize this or not—you have ignored my pain. Sometimes you change the subject when I try to talk about it. Sometimes you respond by telling me about your health problems or doctor appointments as a way of trying to show me you understand.

Although I *do* want to hear about your life and your health, right now I'd like to feel that I have your full attention to what's going on with me.

What I'm saying is I *do* want your nurturing. When I'm in pain, physically or mentally, I want you to notice it, acknowledge it, let me talk about it, listen, and (when you're around) pat me or hold me. It's okay to cry. It's okay to let me know you're sad too. I want you to know I'm still your little girl, wanting her Mama.

I love you,
Linda

Dottie
(Linda's mother)

◈

She told me over the phone that she had cancer. She told me on the eighth of June and on the ninth of June I was here. I kept thinking, "It'll just be in the colon. It'll be all right." But still I came with foreboding. You can't help it.

I had worked with the Cancer Society as a volunteer for about twenty-five years. I thought, "I've paid my dues. She's not going to have any bad effects from this. She's going to be all right."

Then the doctor came down and told us the bad news, that she probably only had months. It was peppered throughout the abdomen and pelvis. Craig and I just grabbed each other and cried.

We knew we had to get hold of ourselves because the doctor said she'd be in recovery in about an hour. I said, "We've got to straighten up, that's all there is to it. We've got to tell her." We didn't know that she was already asking.

She came in on the gurney from the recovery room propped up and reading the pathology report. That did make it a little easier. To me she had a right to know. But then that's the way I feel about me. I have a right to know. Whatever's wrong with my body, I'll deal with it but I want to know about it.

I stayed almost every night with her in the hospital to be sure she was taken care of right. One night I stayed with her friends, Carol and Steve, and I didn't sleep because I was worried about her all night. When I went back the next day, I told Craig, "You need to get back to work. I'll stay here at night and you see to Matt." I said, "I don't sleep if I'm not there anyway."

I kept thinking, "Why couldn't this be me? I'd love to do this for her. I've lived my life. She's too young."

I wished and wished there'd be a miracle, and I prayed and prayed to that effect. She's such a wonderful girl and she's smart. She does so well in her profession. She's got so much to give to the world. Why couldn't it have been somebody else who had nothing to give?

My church has been great. My friends. I have a cousin who's a missionary in Indonesia and he had his church pray. I have a lot of friends and they've all been praying. You can't help but feel that there's a higher power out there.

She and I did a lot of talking after the surgery. Then she came back home, and I felt good about the fact that she came home early. That made me think that she was pretty strong.

Of course my first thought was, "I don't ever want to leave." I can't stand to lose the time with her. Then I thought, "That's not the way her life should be right now. I need to let her have time with her family." The hardest thing I ever did was to go home, but I did go home and get busy. I play bridge a lot, and all of my friends were ready to play bridge with me to keep my mind off it. I came back just before Thanksgiving. Before I came, one of my friends said, "Dottie, be ready. She's probably not going to look the same." I thought she looked tired, but then within two days she looked good again. But when I look at her and think about the bad side, it tears me up. I try to keep hold of myself. It's hard to do. There are times I can't put on an act.

We've always been close. In some ways we are probably closer. I want always to be there for her. And she's always been there for me.

I sort of resent it. I've talked to God about it, that I lost my husband and a few years later, I'm going to lose my daughter. I thought, "This isn't fair."

I had quite a bit of therapy after my husband died because I had some guilt feelings. I learned that you have to accept death, and I better start learning how to do it. I don't want to accept it. Just don't want to.

Janis

As Linda and I talk, she keeps bringing me back to the theme of this book, communication and relationships, and I see more and more how dying throws those issues into bas-relief. It's clear that Linda must cope with more than her own pain and fear; she must also cope with the pain and fear of those she loves. She needs her friends and family desperately, to nurture and reassure and console her. They also need her, to nurture and reassure and console.

Communication and relationships. On a bulletin board in the Intensive Care Unit waiting room at Santa Rosa Memorial Hospital, where my father struggles to survive even though his body is wearing out, a colorful flyer repeats the theme: "Cancer Patients' Support Group Explores Communication and Relationships." My experiences with Linda and with my father are teaching me that dying is a life-changing event, not only for the person who is dying but for those who are part of that person's life. I'm being forced to examine the way I feel about others, not only Linda and my father, but my husband and my children and my mother and my friends. To consider what they mean to me. What I mean to them. At times I am painfully aware of the chasms that exist between me and other people. I have discovered how difficult it is to build bridges in a hurry.

As I watch Linda struggle to cope with the emotional needs of others as well as her own, I see that a desperately ill person needs to re-evaluate what she can legitimately ask of others.

What she can expect from others. It has been difficult for Linda to learn how to ask—and accept—the help she needs, not only from friends and acquaintances but even from her family; in the same way, my mother, almost twice Linda's age, finds it difficult to accept neighbors' offers to drive her forty minutes each way from Sonoma, where she lives, to the hospital in Santa Rosa. She worries about intruding, giving offense, appearing to demand. I try to help her understand one of Linda's early lessons: for some people, giving them the opportunity to help is doing them a service.

I've learned a lot from Linda about communication and relationships, a lot that would be useful to my mother if I could only help her understand. My mother has quietly expressed disappointment that a few of the people she counted as friends have not reached out to her in her time of need; in the same way, Linda felt disappointed and hurt when a few close friends drifted away after she became ill. It was only later that she realized those friendships were grounded in activities that were no longer possible for her. Among other things, Linda has learned that some people know instinctively how to help, and some do not. Some people can cope with others' pain, and some cannot. That's the way it is. "You have to accept people for who they are," she tells me. "You have to tell people what you want and need and let them make up their own minds about what they can do. Let them give what they can give. And don't expect more than that."

Relationships are bound to change when a person is seriously ill. My relationships with both Linda and my parents have changed. When Linda asked me to help write this book, we were primarily business colleagues. In the process of working on the book, we have become friends. Our relationship is now based not primarily on the creative work we did together, where we shared the fun of developing training programs for our clients, but on an intimate sharing of the experience of her illness. If she were to experience a remission, our relationship would change again; I'd like to think it would continue and deepen, but I have no way of knowing whether that would happen. All I know is that it would change.

In the same way, my relationship with my parents has changed since my father became ill. I am no longer child; I am parent. I guide and support my mother as she copes with the pain and fear and confusion, as she faces the prospect of losing her lifelong mate and companion. If by some miracle my father recovers, our relationship will change again, not to what it was before, but to something different.

Communication and relationships. As I watch Linda struggle with her continuing need to care for the emotional needs of her loved ones, I think that the last thing a desperately ill person needs is to be responsible for other people. Yet that is exactly what seems to happen. Linda worries about Craig and Matt and her mother; my father, when he is conscious, worries about my mother worrying about him. Yet I see that the act of worrying, the concern with other people's needs, is often what keeps people connected to this life. What gives people like Linda and my father a reason to hold on as long as they possibly can.

ACCEPTANCE

Riding an Emotional Rollercoaster

※

*I think you experience Elizabeth Kubler-Ross's stages
of acceptance over and over again. Something will
come up and I'll get angry again, or sad again,
or feel acceptance again, or feel shock or denial again.*

I think that I'm so socially trained to rub out my feelings that my way of dealing with feelings is to describe what happened.

When the cancer was diagnosed, I went directly into my work mode. After all the years of conditioning to be a business-woman, I turned to what works for me: I've got a problem, I need to find out as much as I can about it, analyze it, figure out the alternatives, weigh them, select a direction to take, try it, and if it doesn't work, try something else. To me, there's no room for feelings in a business setting. I can't say, "I just kind of feel as if this plan is going to work." I've got to be able to show clients that what I have to offer will address the problem, that they're going to get their money's worth. I can't say, "Gee, I feel real upset that you have this problem, it's really sad." But it didn't take me long to see that this situation is different.

Three months after my first surgery, my CEA count was down. At the time of that surgery, my CEA was in the 200 range.

When I went back to the hospital a month later, it was 40. By mid-September, it was 25.

I asked the doctor, "What does this mean?"

He said, "It could mean that the chemo is helping and we're no longer talking about months."

"Are we talking about a year, two years or what?"

"Let's not get crazy. We'll know more after your next CT scan. But you feel healthy. You look healthy. You are healthy. The chemo is slowing everything down a lot, and hopefully it will even get better."

I was flying. Someone had given me hope. I found myself driving down the street saying, "Thank you, God. Thank you, friends and family, who are helping me and praying for me."

Then I thought about the paradox of having somebody say that you have one or two years to live and have that be good news. The doctor didn't even promise that. He just said, "We'll hope for that." And I thought, "How incredibly sad that I have to think it's great to have one or two years." It was a strange combination of excitement, hope, and sadness.

While I was in Hawaii in August 1992, recuperating from the infection I had in July, I was constantly thinking that my body was dying. I kept wondering if I would spend the rest of my life in and out of the hospital.

When I got back from Hawaii I was exhausted; mentally tired of having to deal with the fact that I was in the last stages of my life. I was starting to live my death instead of my life. And I thought, "I'm tired of this."

Then I read a newspaper article about a woman who was doing a triathalon in which she would swim from Alcatraz to the San Francisco Marina, then ride a bike, and, finally, run a marathon. The previous year, she had had cancer and had been told she had only six months to live, but she had completed the whole triathalon and was getting ready to do it a second time. She had been told that her cancer had completely gone away. I felt so uplifted. I thought, "Linda, you can decide you want to live. You don't have to accept the doctors' prediction that you're going to die. Chemo is helping, and maybe you've got a long life ahead of you."

But two days later, buried in the back section of the paper, I saw the story about how the woman who had done the triathalon had lied about her condition. She had never had cancer. She had changed the story from having overcome depression to having beat cancer. My hopes were completely deflated. I told myself, "You decided you were going to live because of her story and now you find out she was a fraud."

A few weeks later, I thought I felt better. I told my psychiatrist, Dr. Gottfried, "I don't think I'm going to need you for a while because I feel like I'm stabilizing. Everything's about the same, I feel about the same." Then I spent the rest of the time crying in her office over the triathalon woman's lies. It was another one of those times when I realized how delicate my feelings were.

I get mad when people do stupid things that might waste their lives. One night some people near our home were crowded around a car saying goodnight, wearing dark clothing, and standing in the street. If we hadn't seen them at the last second, we would have hit at least five people. I thought, "Why are stupid people still alive? I'm a smart person and I'm dying."

About four months after the initial surgery, I realized I was going through an anger stage. I didn't think I would, but Dr. Gottfried said, "Don't feel bad if you feel like running down people who are walking down the sidewalk looking happy, having a great time when you're having cancer. Don't *do* it, but don't worry if you think about it."

I felt most angry about not having control over when I die. At that time, the doctors were still saying I had a fifty-fifty chance of living one year. To some degree I felt angry about the fact that my cancer was caught so late. Why didn't I feel something going on in my body? Why didn't I report the little things that were bothering me? I felt anger at myself and anger at the doctors and at Craig and at anyone else I might have complained to who didn't force me to go to the doctor.

Our friend Chris Jang, who also has colon cancer, perked me up. He kept telling me, "Don't get too down. There are still miracles out there, and there are still lots of things to do." His cancer had not spread as much as mine. I wanted to help him make the right decisions, select the right doctors and so forth because he seemed to have a good chance for remission, maybe even a cure. I was sort of riding the skirts of his chances, thinking, "If he can get better, I can get better."

One author I read says that you can always hope, but you have to prepare for the worst. I think that's the logical thing to do.

I think I went through all of Kubler-Ross's acceptance stages during the first week. Call it denial or disbelief, part of me kept saying, "I'm really not going to die this year. Look at me. I'm okay. I'm going to make it through this year and I may make it a long time." I also experienced incredible anger. I was so mad that the disease had spread so far without anyone detecting it. I was mad at my doctor, my shrink, Craig, myself, anyone who got in my way. And I bargained: "If I can just have a year, I won't ask for anything else."

Then there was the fearful side: "What if I *am* going to die in a very short time?" I was afraid I couldn't finish things, that I wouldn't have closure, that I would have to leave before I was supposed to, with Matt still to raise and Craig still to be loved and my mother still to see to her end. But at the same time this peaceful, accepting feeling began to emerge: "Everything will be all right, my mother will be all right, Craig will be all right, Matt will be all right, I will be all right."

I've had some of the highest highs of my life during this illness. I've felt incredibly fulfilled and rewarded by the attention I've been given and the love that has come pouring out of people. That part is wonderful. I feel it every day. I've also felt the lowest of the low, waking up in the middle of the night and knowing I really am going to die, but not knowing when, and not knowing how. Not knowing if I'm going to get any warning or if I'll just not wake up one day. Not knowing if I'm going to be able to get through my To Do list.

Judy
(Linda's longtime friend)

Before Linda got sick, we spent a lot of time worrying about what we were doing with our lives. We met about fifteen years ago, when we were coworkers, businesswomen. I stopped working full time when my son was three, just as she began to build her own business.

We had many friendly debates about our different choices. It didn't seem to me that Linda left much time to play. When her cancer was first diagnosed, I told her, "Now you can take time to have fun. We can spend more time together." I think I was trying to find some good in the bad news.

I remember that I was in the kitchen for that awful phone call. She said, "Judy, I'm going to die." I was dumbstruck. I said, "What do you want me to do? Do you want me to come to the hospital?" It was late in the evening, well past visiting hours. She said, "Yes," so I went right away.

It was a struggle to think what I should do; what she would want me to do. She gave me and a few other friends a phone tree to manage. She let me drive her to some doctor appointments. As her illness progressed, I arranged for friends to sit with her when she didn't want to be alone. From time to time, she asked me to help with this book, but I couldn't bring myself to do that while she was still alive.

Doing things for Linda was hard for me. What I wanted was to be with her. I didn't want to control my experience; I just wanted to have it. But she needed to be doing things right up to the end. A peace set in for me when I finally accepted that I couldn't really do anything about her dying. I just had to let it be. And be sad.

One day I was sitting on Linda's bed rubbing her back when her neighbor Diana came over. Diana said something like, "I've heard a lot about you from Linda. What do you do?" I looked her straight in the eye and said, "I'm a humanist." I couldn't believe I'd said that. But at that moment it felt so true. I was a humanist; I was a student of the human condition. Later, we all laughed about how easy it is to mix up what we do with who we are.

I learned so much from watching Linda cope, before and after her illness. After she was diagnosed, two men close to me were identified as at risk for heart disease or cancer because of their Type A behavior. They started in a program of behavior modification to reduce stress, which we now know breaks down the immune system. I couldn't help watching Linda closely. I was afraid to think that maybe she was Type A. Or maybe I was. Terminal cancer is a cruel way to learn to slow down and live.

There's no doubt that Linda's illness changed our relationship. We stopped analyzing the past and making plans for the future. When I was with her I felt as if I had stopped in time, wondering (as the nuns in my grade school would say) what it all meant in the light of eternity.

Clues seemed to be everywhere. One day I bought a book just for the title, *The Sacrament of the Present Moment.* The book cover caught my eye because the painting in my dining room by a friend and woman artist had been reproduced on the cover. Aha, I thought, the present moment *is* sacred. It's all we can be sure of. Another clue came from a phrase on a box of handmade greeting cards, "The greatest art is the art of being alive." I was amazed at how devoted Linda was to living while she was dying.

I finally asked Linda when she thought she would be able to let go. She never answered. And I wondered what drives us all to want more than we have, more of everything, what one author called "the ethics of enough."

My husband always says, "So much to learn, so little time." I learned a lot from how Linda handled her life and her death. I learned the easy way, by watching. The most important thing I learned is to make the most of the moment I'm in. Life is enough, isn't it? After Linda, it's enough for me just to be alive.

Nobody to Blame

I don't ever want to get to the point where I or anyone else blames me for not doing enough. I've done everything I can, and I don't need any guilt trips, especially near the end of my life.

I was incredibly surprised that I had cancer. It wasn't supposed to happen to me. I don't remember ever asking those "Why me?" questions, "I've been a good girl, what did I do to deserve this?" But I do remember thinking, "I've done everything to avoid this; why didn't it work?"

A month after the cancer was diagnosed, I went through my medical records from 1983 up to the present. I don't know what I was looking for—maybe somebody to blame. I wanted to see whether some doctor had missed something, whether I'd ever reported abdominal pain or constipation that might have given a doctor an indication of what I had. But there was nothing to indicate I had ever complained about anything related to my bowel. Doctors typically don't test for colon cancer on an annual basis until age fifty; why should they suggest I have tests when there was nothing to test for? I know I had talked to my doctors about how tired I was, but then I described my lifestyle, working up to twenty hours a day, business projects and deadlines and home and kid and husband. The doctors did what they should have done, based on the information they had, and I did what I thought was right. There was nobody to blame, except maybe myself for waiting so long to complain about how lousy I was feeling.

Also, for a year or two I had been in a black hole of depression. I had spent a year in therapy and was taking Prozac. I had found myself consumed with the idea of death. Dr. Gottfried was monitoring the Prozac, and a psychologist and I were going back through my childhood, trying to crack open some of the secrets.

I hadn't considered suicide, but I was feeling comfortable with the idea of death because it would free me from the dark, gloomy feeling I had a lot of the time. There's a song in *The Phantom of the Opera* about sinking into dark despair, about the gloom and misery of that "black hole" feeling. That's the way I felt, empty and gloomy.

I read about depression and found that other people felt the same way. Rod Steiger wrote a detailed and insightful book about his depression. I also read John Updike's book, *Rabbit is Dead*, about his character "Rabbit" dying. Rabbit doesn't listen to his doctor's suggestions on how to take care of himself and he lets himself die. I felt I was doing that same thing to myself with my work.

A few months before I was diagnosed with cancer, I was cancelling appointments with my psychologist, or delaying them. I had a million excuses, all of them very believable but few of them true. I was busy with work, and I didn't want to slow down. I wasn't sure I was getting all that much help, and I thought, "I can deal with this later." I also delayed or cancelled a couple of appointments with the psychiatrist, and I was always late. Finally, she gave me a lecture. She said, "I think that if you don't stop what you're doing, working such crazy hours and so frenetically and so obsessively, and trying to be perfect and trying to be everything to everybody, that you are going to crash and burn."

I said, "What do you mean by that?"

She said, "Physically. You are going to crash."

I left there in shock. I thought, "What could happen to me? I could have a heart attack. I guess that's what she's talking about." It did put a scare into me. I had never thought about it that way, that I was driving myself to a point of physical exhaustion and perhaps something really serious.

That was about three months before I was diagnosed with cancer. Looking back, I wish I had said to myself, "Listen to these words, and go take care of some of these physical things that are bothering you." I blamed everything on the depression. I wish I'd said, "It's more than just depression. Go find out why you don't feel well. If you have to take the doctor by the throat, demand every checkup in the book." Now I wonder if the cancer caused the depression—or was it the other way around? I think there are a lot of stress factors that inhibit immunity.

But it doesn't do me any good to think I might have caused my own cancer. If I wanted to blame my cancer on something I did, I might come up with a litany of things. But I'm not thinking like that. I think I got colon cancer because it was in my genes; it was part of my chromosomal mix. Mom's dad and all his siblings died of cancer. And somebody in my dad's family passed it along to Dad and me. I didn't give myself cancer from overstressing myself, working too hard, or eating the wrong foods. Anyway, it's too late to do anything differently. It's not as if I can rewind the tape and do it over.

I don't remember ever making a mistake that I couldn't undo, until now. This is the big mistake I can't undo. I don't have control over it. I read in the paper one night that three people died at the Grand Canyon within four days. One was a man who had walked out past the guardrail because he wanted his picture taken on the edge. He slipped and down he went. The other stories were similar, people getting too close to the edge. Craig said, "Can you imagine what goes through your mind at the second you feel yourself falling? You can't take that second back. Probably the only thoughts in your head are, 'Will something save me? Will this turn out to be a dream? Can I turn back the clock a couple of seconds?'"

That's true with this disease, too. There have been times I've thought, "If only I had done this, if only I had pursued this earlier with a doctor, if only a doctor had asked more questions about my bowel habits . . ." But I can't take those seconds back no matter what, so what's the use? It would be a waste of my precious time to spend the rest of my life thinking about the things I could have done differently. If things *had* clearly been a doctor's fault, maybe I would have enjoyed suing him or her. I doubt it, though. Lawsuits take too much energy and cause too much grief. I'd much rather forgive everybody for all the tiny mistakes we made together. That way, I don't blame my doctors, and I don't blame myself.

Exploring Spirituality

*I've become more spiritual. I had never given any credence
to life after death, but now I ask, "Why not?"*

One Friday in September 1992, three months after the cancer diagnosis, Diana told me, "I prayed for you yesterday. I woke up in the morning and started thanking Him for everything I had, and then all of a sudden you came to mind. I said, 'Dear God, Linda needs a miracle, and I ask you to put a light around her whole body and shine your light through her and through every cell of her body.'"

I had been feeling lousy all that week. Monday, I had started feeling nauseous. Tuesday I felt worse, tired and anxious and unable to rest. Thursday I woke up feeling good, and by the end of the day I felt powerful and strong. By Friday, I felt as if I was bursting at the seams with good health. So maybe Diana's prayer did something.

On June 13, 1993, a year after my initial surgery, I joined Christ Presbyterian Church in Terra Linda, California. The church pastors and members have been wonderful to me. I've received an amazing outpouring of love from them.

I had been shopping for a church for a long time, looking for "my" church, one that felt like home. I'd grown up in a church I was very comfortable in, and I longed for that feeling I'd had when I was in the building itself—the people who had made me feel comfortable there and some kind of spiritual essence that was there. I've always felt that if I walked into a church I would know whether the spirit of God resided there. I think it's brought in, or left out, depending upon who goes.

I had that feeling when I went into the Terra Linda Christ Presbyterian church. I felt that spirit was there. I don't mean some fuzzy creature that flies around. Just a sense of acceptance, love, lack of hypocrisy, and openness of mind, not narrowness of view, a feeling that you can believe whatever you want to believe, that you can ask questions. That was important to me. I didn't want to be told what or how to believe, or how to behave.

The pastors of the church will talk with me about spiritual questions on an intellectual basis. I don't get to go to church very often, so they come to my home and we explore some of those questions: What is God, why do people believe in God, what draws people to religion or spirituality, what's the difference between religion and spirituality, what might happen when you die? Is there another dimension? Is there a spirit? A soul?

I've also read books I've really enjoyed. One is called *The Gospel According to Jesus*, by Stephen Mitchell, which takes a historical perspective on what was going on in the world in biblical times and matches it up with what the Bible says was going on. It gives a more realistic view about why writers of the Bible might have said what they said.

I think that Jesus did exist, but whether he was the son of God is open to question. I think he was probably an extremely powerful leader, with a way of verbalizing that appealed to people who didn't have to be intellectual. The uneducated people didn't know how to sit down and talk about the Torah. Jesus interpreted things so people could understand. He also introduced the concept of forgiveness as a way to find peace, forgiving others and forgiving oneself. That's very attractive to me, because I'm so hard on myself. I have a hard time saying, "Hey, you didn't do so great at that, but look what you did do, you don't have to get an A at everything." I can let go more easily if I can forgive myself. I can be extremely judgmental of other people, and I don't want to be like that. I don't want to set standards that someone has to follow in order to be my friend. I think that's why forgiveness is an important theme for me. It allows me more peace to be able to let go.

I also became interested in other beliefs because of the people in my support group and people I seem to have attracted because I'm dying, people who want to talk about spiritual things. Frequently people ask, "Does being this sick make you more interested in what happens after death?" In the beginning, I would say, "no," because it didn't. But because people started asking that question, I started thinking about it, and I started asking what they thought, and I found such a wide diversity of ideas. There are many I'd like to believe are true.

I'd like to believe that there's some system of reincarnation, that we kind of go through levels of perfection and keep coming back until we reach the point of being able to say, "This is it; I don't have to keep coming back any more." But part of me wonders, "How many times do I want to get born again and keep going through all this?" Life is so difficult. Do I have to go through the dying process over and over, too? No, thank you.

I bought a book that is a simplified version of the *Tibetan Book of Living and Dying*. It's called *Letters to a Dying Friend*. The author had begun to develop his spiritual knowledge and he wanted to share these ideas with a friend. His friend kept saying, "You show me some proof and I'll talk to you, but I don't want to talk to you otherwise." Then the friend died suddenly, so the author wrote what he would have liked to have told this person. He explains what he believes happens after you die, where your spirit is and what your spirit is looking for and how you can prepare yourself for dying through meditation. He says that the better trained you are to move your spirit around before death, the easier it will be afterward. That was a little scary. I thought, "I've got to get through this book fast, or I'm not going to know what to do with my spirit once I'm there." I guess I'm supposed to meditate more so I have a greater ability to transport myself outside my body. Have I developed that? No. I still feel I need to practice more. It must not be too great a need, because I don't do it.

At Commonweal, we all seemed to agree there was not a lot of evidence for something after this life, but everybody had had spiritual experiences and wondered what they meant. It was interesting to discuss religion and philosophy, the stuff we used to talk about in high school and college.

One friend who talks with me about spirituality said, "I'm comfortable with whatever death is. It doesn't matter to me whether or not there's life after death; it doesn't matter to me if this whole thing about the light at the end of the tunnel is just the way the brain shuts down. Either way, it's going to be an experience, and that's that. Why get all excited about it? We're all going to go through it."

I thought that was an easygoing way to attack death instead of going into it with fear or anxiety. I've tried to buy into that point of view: Whatever it is, is whatever it is. It would be impossible for me at any point in time to say what I believe, because I just don't know. It's all a mystery and it will be interesting one way or the other to have it resolved.

I did have a strange experience, though. I was having a massage. My massage therapist, Ani Couch, and I were talking about the possibility of an afterlife. I said, "I don't think I believe in it." Ani said, "I wouldn't be so sure about that."

She finished the massage and said, "Why don't you stay and nap for while. I'll wake you in 20 minutes." I felt myself falling asleep, and then I suddenly woke up, knowing that I had been to sleep for a few minutes. I had an overwhelming need to stretch. I stretched my arms out to the side, still with my eyes closed and I thought, "Hmm, Ani's still in the room." I opened my eyes. She wasn't in there. But I thought, "It feels like somebody is in here with me." Then Ani's cat, Bozie, jumped down from the chair where he had been lying on top of my clothes, and started wandering around the room, sniffing and reaching his paw into the air as if he were looking for something, as if he too thought there was something—or someone—in the room with us.

Suddenly I had a feeling that the room was full of people. I felt that my grandpa Sam, who was my closest male support during my childhood, was standing next to me. Next to him was my grandmother, and next to her were my other grandparents. I felt as if a line of people extended out of the room into infinity, and all the faces were looking at me, sending me a message: "We're here, and we're with you." Then it was over, and Bozie went back to his chair.

I think I had a peek into the other side. I told Ani I thought I'd spent a few minutes in the Twilight Zone. She said, "Maybe there is an afterlife, Linda."

I said, "I'm not sure but I think I'll give it some more thought."

Rev. David Steele
(Linda's pastor)

Linda first came to Sunday worship with Marty, a woman around Linda's age and a seminary student. Linda had evidently been looking around, and she had passed several churches on the way here.

I asked, "What are you doing here?" In response, she wrote a short article for our church paper. Essentially it said, "As a Yuppie, I lost track of church, as most of my generation has. And now I'm discovering that I want to get refocussed on what it was all about." She wrote, "I'm home." It was the image of home she used.

She told me, "You've got such a great thing here, you ought to market it better."

I said, "What is it we've got to market? What did you see here?"

So she wrote that piece.

I kept saying, "If you get better, let's market this thing; I think you could put us on Easy Street, with all your energy." That was the beginning.

She joined the church on the first anniversary of the day the doctor sewed her up and said, "You've got six months to live." It turned out that she had six months after that, and then another year and then more.

One of the things she was tied into here is something called the Stephen Ministry. We have some people who go through quite an extensive training period to become active listeners, who share one-on-one relationships with others. It's a caring ministry, not a curing ministry, based on the biblical Stephen, who was the first deacon. The deacons have always been those people who are particularly concerned with the poor and the sick and so forth.

Judy Hubbard was Linda's Stephen Minister. On Judy's first visit, Linda said, "Now, let's work out what it is I expect from you and what it is you expect from me." So, at the very beginning, it was clear what the arena was. Most of us aren't that clear.

I think that her whole sense of mortality, her sense that she only had a little time, meant she was going to use that time. She wasn't going to waste it if she could help it. It tended to push her forward into something that the rest of us might shilly-shally around with for three or four different meetings. There are two kinds of directness. There's a kind of attacking directness, a sort of belligerent directness . . . I never picked that kind up from Linda. I didn't feel I needed to fuss around and be nice to her and stuff like that. When I talked with her, I could talk turkey, go in there and say, "Okay, now what's up?" and we'd get at it.

People look for a rootedness in some way or other. And people find rootedness in different ways in America today. Evidently Linda's childhood experience in the church was a positive one, and so she had the feeling that there was some kind of nourishment there. I think there are points in your life where your sense of control, that sense of, "I'm running this," is questioned. It can come in many ways: divorce does it, any kind of ailment does it, losing your job does it. The church is one place people go when that happens. People also go into all kinds of New Age stuff, into 12-step programs, to many different places. You wonder if anything is solid when life is slipping out of your hands.

I think of it as searching for roots. Here's a tree, and you're getting blown over. That was one of the images Paul Tillich used, that God is up to something here. God is the depths. God is the Ground of Being. So that as you go deeper into the self, as you go deeper into whatever is, you are getting close to God.

Of course, Linda was not one to give up control. In fact, at the very end she was trying to control everybody and everything. She had a five-hour funeral she was ready to put on. It would have taken forever. I used to tell her, "You're going to have to limit this." If she could have, she would have been there directing the whole thing. That was the fun thing about it for her, working everything out.

Linda knew who she was and she could only be who she was. Who else can you be? If you've lived in control for forty-five years, you're not going to sit around and twiddle your thumbs. I think there are some positive things in life that grow out of this rootedness. There's a lot of strength that grows out of the depths. I would say that courage is a spiritual value, the power to stick it out. She'd keep saying, "You know, I look at my body, and I look in the mirror, and I shouldn't be here. But I wake up in the morning and I decide to live, and so I just do, for another day. I've got things to do, and so I do them."

I think life is holistic. I think Linda had that sense of centeredness, including a safe space to raise questions and howl if you want to and say, "What do I believe and what don't I believe?"

I think of Socrates saying in that beautiful death passage of his, "Well, maybe it's just a long eternal sleep, but I've had many wonderful nights' sleep, so if it's just eternal sleep, that's fine. And maybe there's something else on the other end, and so it doesn't really matter." It isn't like believing or not believing is essential. But I find its very hard to stand at a grave or to be a part of a life that's gone and not sort of instinctively sense that there's something vital that was a part of this person and it must be somewhere. I think it's very hard to say, "Well, that was that." So I think people do believe there is life beyond the grave, whether they get it together intellectually or not. There's something in the heart that insists it be that way.

More and more, I don't think what we believe matters that much. I mean, do you believe in electricity? You operate on certain assumptions. And faith is trust, more than belief. The life of faith has a believing angle in it, but essentially it's trusting. I think that was where Linda was. She did succeed in letting go of some of her need to run everybody's life.

One of the things I would kid her about was, "What if you don't die nobly? So what?" She'd laugh. She'd say, "I have to die nobly." I told her that my dad's final words were, "Change the furnace filters." I think in this day and age when we know so much about Hospice and dying, people tell valiant tales of folks dying, and the pressure to die well is almost worse than the pressure to live well. Once I wrote a poem about it. I said: I'm going to get the essence of my philosophy of life down so that in my final words, as my family gathers around, I'll be able to tell them the meaning of life. But what if I forget it? So I'll write it down on a three-by-five card. Then just as I get ready to pick up that card the nurse will have taken away my glasses and I won't be able to read the card. So as my family gathers over me, I say something like, "Get that damn tube out of my nose," and then I kick off. So what if you don't die nobly? Don't people have a right to howl at the end or have their final words be, "Get this tube out of my nose"?

Somebody defined ritual as what you do when you can't focus enough to do anything else. In grieving, it's very, very clear that there has to be some concrete way of recognizing that a person is really dead. I remember one time when I was chaplain at Punahou School in Honolulu, a girl graduated, went off to Colorado, fell off a horse, got kicked in the head, and died, and there was nothing in the paper, and there was no funeral because the family were Christian Scientists. Her classmates came around and they said, "We can't believe she's dead. We've got to have something." So we set up a memorial in the chapel where these kids could get together and, in a ritual, remember her and honor her, and then allow the closure that the mind and heart crave.

Marin County is full of people who don't want any memorial service. That's awful. That's the biggest blow you can give your

family, to prohibit them from honoring you and remembering
you. It's the worst present somebody could leave to their family.
Yet people do it all the time and think they're being noble. That's
one request you should never honor. The service isn't for the
dead person, it's for the living. Whatever it is, it allows things to
be said. It allows the mind to begin to think. And then there's the
remembering and the honoring and the beginning of closure.
Jesus said, "Blessed are they that mourn, for they shall be com-
forted," and we know that's literally true, that it is in the grieving
that the healing comes, and if you don't grieve, then the scab
forms over the hurt and it comes up in some strange ways psychologically. In the telling of the stories is the healing.

When somebody's died and you're seeing the spouse or whoever for the first time, you wonder, "What do I say?" The answer
is quite simple. You just ask, "How did they die?" You ask the person to tell you the story of their loved one's dying, and then soon
you've joined in and you're telling stories together.

There are two things we want to do: honor people and
remember them, and then wish them well on their journey. Let
them go. I think as we let them go, healing takes place. But it
takes a long time. Any time you have a chance to be with somebody in this kind of a situation, it's a deeply meaningful
experience.

I wrote my thesis on Odgen Nash. Clifton Fadiman said that
portentous literature deals with the highs and the lows of human
life, about 10 percent of human experience. Ogden Nash was the
poet of the other 90 percent. He wrote about ordinary stuff,
whether you should shave before you shower or after you shower,
about things he noticed with his children. He was paying attention. That's always interested me, how there are some people
who do pay attention. It interests me that when people talk about
God in their lives, they either talk about high moments or low
moments, "When I had my baby" or "I was sick" or something
like that. But what about all these in-between moments? Linda
began to be aware of all those moments and began to live in
those moments. It's pretty nice, every now and then, to realize we
can actually be living while we're alive.

One thing I try to do is get clear with somebody, "What do
you want me to be?" When we are dying, we need one or two

people with whom we can be whoever we are at the time. Then the rest of the people are people you can deal with . . . nobly or something. I think Linda had several people with whom it didn't matter what she said, whether she was up or down or whatever.

Every friend can't be in that inner circle. Some people want me, as the minister, in that circle, and some don't. With Linda, I could show up and she wouldn't have to worry about being strong. It's a privilege to be in that position. It doesn't happen all that often.

In these relationships, I don't try to be serious or "religious." What happens is, today we may horse around. Tomorrow is a down day and maybe we just sit together. Then there are times we focus on, "Well, now, what are you going to do? Are you going to get cremated?" Okay, that's over. "Who won the ball game?" Sometimes we want to live. A person doesn't want to sit around dying all the time.

A "Celebration of Life" Party

I decided to have a party on June 12, 1993—an anniversary party, a big celebration that I had survived for a year, that I beat the odds. I really wanted to do this for myself, to surround myself with people who mean something to me. The list kept getting longer and longer and longer. I'll celebrate every June 12th that I get!

Several years ago, I visualized a party in my home. In the vision, I had on a white dress and my house was filled with the hum of people I loved and who loved me. It was a celebration of my retirement from my current career, my way of saying, "That part of my life is over and I'm going to start something new." I was handing the business over to the people who came to my house. "Take it— go and prosper."

I felt the June party was that dream coming true, although in a different way than I had planned. First, it was a celebration of life, because I had lived one year to the day since my initial cancer surgery. Second, it was to thank people for the incredible amount of support and encouragement they had given me during that first year and during my lifetime.

Some of the people Craig and I invited were people who hadn't been in our lives that year, but they had in some way helped to enrich our lives at other times. There were a few people who hadn't contacted me, maybe because they were scared. I was a little resentful about some of those people until I sat down to make the party list. Then I thought, "I can give that up. I can realize that these people had an impact on my life at some point, maybe not this year, but that's okay." Other people only came into my life that year and I wanted them to feel thanked and recognized.

Third, we wanted to help people become aware of how important every day is. Maybe they won't get it any other way than from seeing how important it is to me. That's why we worded the invitation the way we did.

We sent out ninety-six invitations, mostly to people in the Bay Area. I thought about the fact that the invitees fell into categories. There were people I had worked with at Shaklee and Learning International, colleagues who had worked for and with me on consulting projects, Craig's professional friends, people Craig plays tennis with, people we had met through the neighborhood and Matt's school.

When people come to a party this size, they usually find the host or hostess or somebody they know, and stay in one group. They don't usually connect with new people with whom they may have something in common. I wanted people to have a way to start a conversation. I hired some greeters, and when people arrived, a greeter led them to a table with name tag stickers that had descriptions on them: "Guitar Player," "Couch Potato," "Trainer." The guests picked out tags that described them, or made their own. As they walked around, they could go up to someone and say, "Hey, you really saw a UFO?" Or, "I play

You, our family and friends,
Have brought us love, joy, and encouragement
During our lives,
And especially this past year.

We want to thank you from our hearts
And celebrate the blessing of life
And the gift of each day.

Please join us at our open house
Saturday, June 12, 1993

Craig, Linda, and Matthew Mukai

guitar, too," or "I'm a jazz musician." I also wanted people to leave with a living reminder of why we had had this party, so we gave each person a potted plant with a message about living attached to it. I hired a pianist and a photographer. I wanted my picture taken with every person at the party, so I could make a big album to look at later. The reality of the party was that it was in lieu of a funeral, only I got to be there.

Although I had been in a lot of pain for several weeks, I had a lot of stamina the day of the party. I was hyped up, excited, although I was constantly running back to the bathroom and plugging down a painkiller. I told the food service people not to offer me food because I was afraid I would get nauseous.

With 130 people here over a four-hour period, I figured that I got to spend less than two minutes with each person. I wanted to talk to everybody, and I didn't want anyone to leave. I found myself wanting to block the door and say, "Don't leave. I want this to last longer!"

A lot of people did stay until 9:00, and a few stayed until 9:30 or so. Then everybody was gone except family and overnight guests. We stayed up until midnight debriefing the party and it was really fun. The amazing thing was that I was never tired. I was running on reserves, I guess, but it was wonderful.

During the next few weeks, I had the feeling that everyone was standing outside the house holding hands. I could still hear the voices and the music, and I had this wonderful feeling of love and joy and happiness. I want to remember it all, the array of faces circling around me and each other, the sound of cheerful voices, music in the background. It's not something I have to do again even if I live five or ten more years, but it was so special, it will be preserved in my memory forever.

I sent a thank-you note to everybody who came and to people who had been invited but couldn't come and sent flowers or notes. I felt that the party was some kind of closure for me, because I probably won't see many of the people who were there again. I felt it was a good ending, a retirement of sorts. I felt as if I were letting go of some people, concentrating instead on a few and asking myself who would be in that final circle around my bed.

<hr/>

June 29, 1993

Dearest Family and Friends,

It's been two weeks since our party and since then I've had surgery, resumed treatment with a portable IV that pumps chemo into my body twenty-four hours a day, started wearing a pain control patch, and taught a two-day seminar. Life truly does go on!

Please forgive us for sending this generic thank-you note. Thanks to all of you who came to our Celebration of Life party and to you who sent your well wishes. The house still rings with your voices, the music and the "joie de vivre."

We appreciated your presence, and to those of you who brought or sent presents (tsk, tsk—this was not supposed to be a gift occasion), we appreciate the beauty and thoughtfulness of those too. Due to our disorganization, the presents were often separated from their cards and we are not sure who brought what. We ask your forgiveness for not acknowledging you properly and hope you will feel free to tell us what to thank you for!

Exactly one year before the party, June 12, 1992, I underwent the surgery that removed a foot of my colon and a few lymph nodes. The doctors said that colon cancer had metastasized throughout my abdomen and pelvis and that they could not promise us even one year. (My dad was diagnosed with colon cancer one month later and given the same prognosis.) Well, obviously, we made it and hope to keep the doctors stupefied for many years to come.

We give the credit for this year not merely to medical science, but to all the attention, love, support, and prayers of our friends and family. The party was our way of thanking you, as well as creating the memory of so many of you in one place at one time.

Being a born consultant and trainer, I want to share with you some startling facts, some unpleasant advice and some loving thoughts:

Startling Facts

- 1 out of 3 people get cancer in their lifetime.
- 120,000 people in the U.S. get colon cancer and 60,000 die from it each year.
- The typical test for colon cancer (a stool sample) misses 70% of cases.
- The Cancer Society's warning signal for colon cancer is "change in bowel habits," but it should include bowel problems over a lifetime.
- Colon cancer can be cured if caught before it metastasizes.

Unpleasant Advice

- Listen to your body, relate to your doctor even the tiniest complaints, and never hesitate to ask your doctor to perform more than the standard physical exams (to thoroughly check for colon cancer, you need a sigmoidoscopy and a barium enema or a colonoscopy. I warned you that this was unpleasant!).
- Don't let your work consume your time so much that you delay or cancel medical exams.

Loving Thoughts

Treat every day as a lifetime:
greet each morning as a new beginning,
choose the ways you will spend your time,
expect change,
create memories,
give and receive love,
look for beauty,
forgive yourself and others,
leave no unfinished business, and
appreciate the end,
as it gives meaning to it all.

Thanks again, dear ones.

Linda, Craig, and Matthew

Living Without a Future

After a few months, I noticed that people were beginning to imagine life going on without me. I had encouraged that kind of talk. I had said, "I want you to say whatever you're thinking and not worry about it." It was still very shocking. Very hurtful. I realized that people were beginning to accept the reality of it.

On TV one night, there was a show about life spans, how much scientists are learning about DNA in order to slow down the aging process. They think that within the next decade they may have solved the mystery of aging. People could choose to be a hundred or two hundred years old—or more! I thought, "I don't want to live *that* long. But I would like to see my sixties."

It began to bother me that everybody had a future to discuss and I didn't. During our Valentine's Day dinner in February 1993, Craig said, "I don't think I'll ever get married again. No one could ever live up to what you are as a wife and a partner."

I said, "Ah, so you're thinking about it, huh?" Then I said, "I would want you to find another partner. I think you need to have a partner."

He said, "I could see myself having relationships, but I couldn't see myself getting married. What reason would there be? I don't want any more children and to me that's the only reason to get married."

I said, "I don't want you to have just a 'relationship.' Find somebody and commit to her. Unless you commit to her by getting married, you won't make it work." That's the way we did it. We got married, and we made it work.

We talked about all that for a while. Then I became uncomfortable. I said, "You know, I really don't want to talk about your future wives and lovers any more. I'm not dead yet."

One weekend, a visiting relative said to me, "Craig says he wants to retire in five years." That was a surprise. I thought, "He's planning his retirement without even talking to me about it."

Later, while Craig was putting Matt to bed, she asked, "Do you think Craig would ever move?" I didn't know what to say in response except, "Craig loves our home. I don't know what he'll do in the future." Later, Craig and I talked about it, and he assured me that he hadn't been planning his retirement without me. But I could understand why he would think about such things, so I asked him to discuss it with me when he was ready.

A couple of months later we were at dinner with some friends and the conversation turned to retiring, transition careers, and the future. I got upset, and I ended the evening as soon as we finished dessert. I remember saying, "I'm tired, let's go." It was only about nine o'clock. I wasn't angry with anybody, but I remember thinking, "Gosh, this isn't fair." Looking back, I see I missed an opportunity to say to those friends, "It's fun to talk about your futures, but I feel left out." I'm sure everyone would have responded well, and we would have been able to continue with our evening.

No Longer Independent

❧

I've been working to pay my own way since I finished high school. Now I'm working maybe one day a week, if that, and not making what I would consider my share of the family's income. It's difficult for me to think about Craig shouldering the whole burden. And it's not just the money, it's the dependency.

One night I dreamed that Craig came to me and said, "Look, it's not you and it's not Matt, but I've got to be out on my own. I'm leaving you." I woke up with a start. All of a sudden it dawned on me how dependent I am. In the dream, I thought, "What am I going to do? I'll have to work and I don't feel like working with cancer. Where will I live? Who's going to take care of me when I'm sick?" I could still make it on my own, but it would be miserable.

In another dream, Craig was having an affair with another woman. I was very angry. It wasn't just the betrayal, it was also the fact that when I needed him the most, I had to leave him.

I completely trust Craig and I'm not concerned about his going off with another woman. We talked about the dream, and what it really came down to was that I felt this overwhelming need for him. On the one hand, it's improved our relationship, but it also scared me because I realized I depend on him now for my half of the income, for personal support, for help with child care, for help around the house.

I also felt the dream was about the fact that I have no choice but to let him go at some point. If I die—when I die—I will have to let him go and there will be other women, in time.

A few weeks later, I went with my friend Mary Edwards to see *The Cemetery Club*, a movie about three widows. All of a sudden I had a brainstorm. I whispered to Mary, "I just had an 'aha.' Can I tell you about it?" There were only about ten people in the theater.

I said, "What I just realized is that in letting go of this need for independence, I can also let go of this need for responsibility. For the first time in my life, I can do something irresponsible." I've been acting responsible since I was old enough to walk. Now nobody can depend on me. The consultants who have been working with me are no longer dependent on me for income. Craig is not dependent on me to meet the monthly bills. My friends don't expect much from me anymore. My mom has to depend on herself. It was very exciting to think about doing something irresponsible, except that I couldn't come up with any irresponsible things to do. Out of practice, I guess.

A few weeks after that, Craig told me, "You don't need to feel that you have to do your share. You earned a lot of money, and we have been able to accomplish a lot of things, provide for our future and our child's future. You're done with that. You don't have to make money anymore."

I said, "This problem is in my head. It's not in my checkbook. It's giving up a whole part of me."

He said, "Why can't you still consider yourself independent? If something happened to me tomorrow, you would still be fine. We have built enough together that you would never have to work again. Can't you still feel that you and Matt would get along just fine?" There is no end to this man's love and support for me. I just have to learn to accept it.

The Happiest Year of My Life

❧

*Craig and I were sitting on the side of the bed one night
talking about some friends who were having marital problems.
I said, "I love them both so much, I really want them to be able
to work this out. It's so sad that everybody can't be as happy
as we are." And then we started to laugh.*

In three different places in my hospital records I was referred to
as an "unfortunate forty-six-year-old woman." I thought, "Why
do people refer to me as unfortunate?" As if it had to do with luck
that I got this disease. As miserable as I've felt sometimes in my
life, I still feel like a very fortunate person. Even with cancer I
don't feel like an *un*fortunate person.

After my diagnosis, I felt some regret because I wasn't going
to be able to finish my work, complete some of my creative projects. I wouldn't be able to succeed in my business because I
would have to stop working. Then I had an immediate after-
thought—relief. I realized I no longer had to prove anything to
anybody, because I'd already succeeded. I could stop working
and still feel proud of myself.

Oddly enough, when the cancer was diagnosed, the depression I'd felt during the preceding year was over. I stopped having
those black, empty feelings, even though I finally had something
to be depressed about. In fact, the year after my surgery was the
happiest of my life. Craig and I realized we had everything in the

world to be grateful for: our deep, enduring love, our son, our families, our home, our work. We just had this one horrifying thing happening to us. But we had changed the way we looked at things, we enjoyed everything in the moment, we were happy to be together, we stopped to smell the roses, and we realized that we were surrounded by love.

Cancer has prompted us to do things and say things we wouldn't have otherwise. I've had the chance to tell people I love them, to say goodbye, to be loved and cared for. We had no idea we had so many friends and that we were so important to our families. This, to me, is what life is all about: loving people and being loved.

Janis

There is a strong theme in the interviews I conducted while putting together this book: "Linda is too good a person to die." I agree. I think there are good people and not-so-good people, and Linda is one of the best, a rare individual who harbors no malice towards others, a caring, sharing, thoughtful person with a gentle, funny, positive energy, the kind of energy we need more of in this complicated world.

Talking with her one day in April 1993, I was struck by how well she looked, how much energy she seemed to have. At the same time, I had a sense that she had become less . . . substantial. That's not the right word. What I mean is she seemed somehow less connected to the world in which I lived. A subtle shift seemed to have taken place in the way she related to people and events, as if she had taken a step back and had separated everyone into two groups: in one group were people with cancer like herself and her father, and in the other group, everyone else.

It was not surprising that Linda now perceived the world differently. That she had cancer, that she faced the imminence of her own death, informed her every choice. Her full-time job had become finding a way to survive, coping with what she needed to do to her body in order to survive. I thought that the behavior of the rest of us must seem increasingly strange, our priorities a little ridiculous. It was as if she had found herself living on an island linked to the mainland by a bridge that was coming apart. When I tried to articulate my impressions, my husband said it sounded as if Linda was preparing to die. I agreed at first, but later I saw that we were wrong. Linda was not preparing to die. She was preparing for life, but for a life changed by her cancer.

As that spring progressed toward summer, Linda began to focus on her "Celebration of Life" party, tackling it the same way she tackled her business projects, with her full attention. One day she told me that she was happier than she had ever been in her life. Her face glowed when she talked about how much closer she and Craig had become. Interesting, I thought, the way people are often at their best in a crisis. Maybe it takes a crisis to bring us to attention.

The party was a great success. The weather was perfect, the house was beautiful, the food was great, and everyone had a good time. There was a wonderful mix of people, many of whom were close to Linda, and others who had only a tangential relationship. Her mother was there, of course, and Craig's family; her friends Diana, Sue, and Judy; some of Craig's dentist friends and tennis partners; Carolyn Balling, a longtime business associate and friend; and many others, most of whom I didn't know. Linda looked beautiful, happy, and relaxed. There was no sign that for weeks she had been struggling with increasing amounts of pain. I wasn't sure whether we were there to congratulate her on making it through a year, or to say goodbye. Maybe it was a little of both. Maybe we needed toasts: "Here's to Linda, one year forward."

PREPARATION

A Turn for the Worse

❦

*A month after my party, Dr. Spivack wrinkled up his face
and said, "Linda, you're worse." That was the first time
he said anything to me that wasn't in the most positive light.
He was very serious, and I knew things looked bad.*

Just after my "Celebration of Life" party, Dr. Spivack asked me to
see my gynecologist, Dr. Jeanette Brown. During a pelvic exam,
he had felt a lump, and he wanted her to feel it. I said I wanted to
see a urologist, too. I was having a lot of pain in my right pelvic
area, and I felt something was wrong with my urology system. Dr.
Spivack said, "Do both."

My urologist, Dr. Harry Neuwirth, sent me for an ultrasound test that indicated I had a kidney stone, or scar tissue, or a
tumor blocking my right ureter. He scheduled a procedure called
a cystoscopy for the next day. A cystoscopy is one of those procedures that sends women skidding up the wall. I saw a cartoon
once with a woman wearing one of those silly gowns tied in the
back. She's on an examining table standing straight up in the stir-
rups, and the doctor's saying, "Mrs. Jones, the first thing you
need to do is relax!" That's what the procedure reminded me of.

The night before the cystoscopy, I had even more pain in my
side and in my bladder. When I got to the hospital, I told Dr.
Neuwirth about the pain during the night, and he sent me for a

special X-ray called an IVP. The IVP indicated that no blockage existed. Dr. Neuwirth didn't know whether I had passed a stone in the night or the ultrasound had been read incorrectly. But he decided to go ahead with the cystoscopy because I was still experiencing a lot of pain. During the procedure, they found a new tumor that had adhered to my pelvic organs and was too large to remove.

Every day I was getting increasing amounts of pain, stabbing pains in my abdomen and pelvis, sometimes in my ribs, even down my thigh. I worried about what the pain meant. The doctor said it could be cancer cells around the nerves, inflammation, scar tissue, or a number of other possibilities. It scared me. One night I was afraid to let myself fall asleep because I felt as if my chest were compressed. I asked Craig to sit up with me. I wanted him to watch me because I was afraid that when I fell asleep I'd stop breathing. Craig sat with me and stroked my head; he told me I was breathing well, my pulse was fine and I was going to be okay. Finally, I went to sleep.

I felt so tired from the pain. None of the painkillers helped. I'd go to sleep, but I'd wake up every hour. I'd look at the clock and think, "Oh, only one hour has gone by!" They were giving me Naprosyn, which is an anti-inflammatory, and Tylenol with codeine. I was taking it so often that Craig was afraid I would get hooked on the codeine. I also tried Vicodin, but it didn't help much either. Later Dr. Spivack started me on a pain patch, Fentanyl. I was taking so many painkillers I couldn't remember what I had said five minutes earlier.

By the end of August, the pain had become so serious that I had to start taking morphine tablets. The doctors explained that when you take morphine for pain, you don't get the strange side effects associated with the drug, and even high levels may not make you groggy. It's different than taking it as a recreational drug. It took me several weeks to get accustomed to it. At first I felt sleepy and a little drunk, then I stabilized. Later, when I needed more, Dr. Spivack consoled me by saying I was still on a low dose and we could go even higher.

The pain was a constant reminder that the cancer was there. There's also a psychological aspect to taking morphine: I felt as if

I must be close to death, because people sometimes assume disease is serious when you have to take morphine. I called my mom and asked her to come take care of me for a while—I was afraid to be on my own with the morphine, the pain, and the fear of death.

After a CT scan that showed growth in all my tumors, Dr. Spivack referred me to a radiation oncologist, Dr. Richard Evans, to see whether radiation could shrink the pelvic tumors. Craig and I went to see him. We took my friend and neighbor, Nancy Lurmann, who also had colon cancer.

I wasn't ready for what Dr. Evans had to say. He suggested twenty-five radiation treatments, five each week for five weeks. The side effects included fatigue, nausea, more frequent bowel movements, diarrhea, bladder irritation, red, sore skin, and other discomforts. He said the side effects would begin during the last couple of weeks of the radiation and continue for about five weeks afterwards. I would lose hair only on the area being radiated.

It was the risks that caused me the most concern. Dr. Evans said there was a risk of perforating the bowel. It wouldn't necessarily happen right away; it could happen months later. That would be very serious because the bowel would spill into the pelvic area, causing an infection that would be fatal.

Another risk was a fistula. A fistula is like a canal that could be created between the rectum and vagina or between the bladder and vagina so that excretions would be discharged out of the vagina. That seemed abhorrent to me. Dr. Evans also said that the tumor itself could cause a perforated bowel or a fistula. We wouldn't know whether they were caused by radiation or the tumor.

After radiation, the tumor could begin to grow again immediately, and they can't radiate the same area twice. Dr. Evans reminded me that my liver was still at risk because of a tumor there, and I could have liver malfunction at any moment. And he said that the cancer had probably begun or would begin shortly to metastasize to another major organ—lungs, brain, or kidneys.

I said, "It sounds as if I don't have much time."

He said, "You don't. You might have six months. A six-month period of living day to day, not knowing what's going to happen to you. Any of these things could happen immediately."

That wasn't what I'd expected to hear. I had come there to decide whether I wanted to have radiation treatments. I hadn't come to hear how short my lifespan was or how I was going to die. It was overwhelming. Scary. Disappointing. I'd thought I had at least another year. Things had seemed so rosy in December, and why they turned around the way they did, I didn't know.

I had to say to Dr. Evans, "I'm sorry but I don't have any more questions. I may have some later but I have to get out of here right now." Nancy and Craig asked some questions, but we were really struck by the seriousness of it all.

As I was leaving, I said, "If I had the choice of pulling the plug, I would pull it now."

Dr. Evans said, "You do have that option now, Linda. You have the option of turning down radiation and going off chemo and letting nature take its course."

It would be very rapid. But it wasn't an option I could seriously consider, not then. I still felt pretty good, and I still had too many things to do. My To Do list was still too long. In the end, I decided I had no choice but to begin the radiation.

The first step was a "radiation simulation." I had to lie on the radiation table while the technicians mapped out the area they were going to radiate. It took them a day or two to build the lead blocks they use to keep radiation from hitting areas the doctor wants to exclude. Then I went back to try the blocks on, to make sure everything was right. They tattooed dots on my pelvis and abdomen so they could line my body up the same way each time.

I was nervous going in there. It was starting another "something" and I didn't know what to expect, whether it would help me or hinder me. Each treatment took sixty seconds on each side, front and back. I would lie there and count, "One one-thousand, two one-thousand. . . ." It wasn't painful. There was no sensation at all. Sometimes I visualized the radiation beams burning away the cancer and leaving nice, pink, healthy tissue.

After only a few treatments, however, the pelvic tumor caused a bowel obstruction. I was up all night, taking enemas, laxatives and stool softeners, trying to get some action out of my colon.

Craig walked me around the house, again and again, hoping exercise would help. But nothing worked. I was bent over in pain when I finally gave in and called Dr. McAuliffe, who told me to go to the hospital to see if they could loosen me up. The enemas they gave me did nothing; I went home and waited for morning, praying that there were ways to unblock me that weren't painful.

The next morning we called Dr. McAuliffe to find out what to do. He said to meet him at Marin General so he could examine me and make a recommendation. I was scared to death.

Dr. McAuliffe confirmed that a tumor had compressed my colon, and he said that there was nothing he could do. He thought my only chance was a colostomy or other surgery that would bypass the blockage. We were going to have to make another very difficult decision.

Nancy Lurmann

Dear Linda,

I'm so sorry you had to get that earful and heart-load of information from the radiation oncologist yesterday. You must have been wrecked yesterday and last night.

I want to say that I love you and care about your psyche, soul, and body, and that I will support you in whatever you want to do about medical or nonmedical treatment. If you decide to go for radiation, I will happily drive you there three times a week. It is never a burden to help you or a difficulty (physically) for me to be with you. Our time is limited and I am selfish about wanting to be with you during my ending processes. My parole might be a bit longer, but my death sentence has been sounded, too (based on rampant cancer inside my ovary, on the outside of my other ovary, and on my bladder).

I also want to say that if you decide to forgo the radiation treatments, that is not giving up the fight. It is surrendering to the fact that a medical intervention will not have any long-term effect on the quality (here I go, using that awful cancer cliche) and quantity of your life. You are not a wimp if you "just say no" to an oncologist. In fact, I think it takes more courage to say, "Enough, boys, your high-tech toys and poison potions aren't going to cut it any longer."

Should you decide to go for treatments, Dr. Evans is a *mensch*—except for the fact that he issued a death sentence. When will these people learn that people like you don't fall into the statistical norm in any way, shape or form? Your six months might really be two years and six months. My one to two years might be eight months.

I'm going to San Francisco to see David's sister this morning. I'll also go to Spivack's to get unplugged [from the continuous infusion] and have the illusion that I'm normal for a few moments.

Love, Nancy

Question Authority!

❧

I feel like I have to question everything. I can never turn my life over to someone else to make my decisions for me.

When Dr. McAuliffe told us he thought I needed surgery to unblock my colon, we asked him to contact the colorectal surgeon who had performed my initial surgery, a lifetime ago in June 1992. He made the call and said the surgeon would call us back to advise us. Craig and I waited in the hospital room for his call.

The surgeon finally called back at 9:45 p.m. saying he'd had car problems and hadn't been able to call until then. Craig and I had been worrying all day long about what was going to happen.

Craig took the phone call. I saw a cloud cross his face, and I knew it was very bad news.

The surgeon told Craig that if a colostomy or any surgery was done, I would not heal, I would be in horrible pain, and I would die a painful death in two to three weeks. The surgeon's best recommendation was to stop feeding me and keep me "comfortable" until I died. It would be the "humane" way.

Before Craig could relate the conversation to me, I went into the bathroom. I frequently do that when I need time to collect my thoughts. When I had composed myself, I came back out and said, "I know what you're going to tell me. He says 'no' to the surgery. But I'm not ready to give up. I feel too good. I'm not going to die. Except for this one thing, I'm fine." Maybe it was naive to believe that the only thing wrong with me was a plumbing problem. But how could I choose death?

Craig said, "Let's find another surgeon. These options are unacceptable." I knew Craig was thinking, "I don't want to give her too much hope." But I knew that whatever I wanted to do would be okay with him. We called our internist, Dr. Oppenheim, at home, even though it was late. Craig said, "Al, get us somebody else as soon as possible; we need someone who can do the surgery." Dr. Oppenheim referred us to Dr. Mark Bazalgette, who performed the colostomy the next day. I healed quickly and thoroughly.

The incident had frightening implications. I thought, "What about people who are not assertive enough to relate their wishes, or whose upbringing conditioned them to believe that the doctor is always right?" Even people who manage their own lives well often defer to the authority of people with "M.D." after their names.

When I am with doctors, I remind myself that I am the one ultimately responsible for my health and well-being. I have to make sure that I completely understand what they tell me—not just pretend to understand—and that I get all my questions answered. Without a clear understanding of my illness and my treatment choices, I can't apply my priorities and make a good decision.

Looking back, Craig and I thought that the surgeon who made the first recommendation made several professional errors. He demonstrated a lack of concern for people in a crisis—he could have asked someone in his office to call us earlier that day to let us know he was having difficulties getting back to us, and that we had not been forgotten. Instead, he seemed to have ignored us for more than eight hours, while we dealt with the gravest of worries and fears.

He had also assumed an all-knowing position from which to view my case. He had only spoken to Dr. McAuliffe over the phone and had not seen any scans or current reports on me. In fact, he hadn't examined me for more than eighteen months, yet he apparently felt that he could predict my current condition and determine my treatment options.

When he finally called, he coldly stated that my choices were to have surgery to unblock my colon and die painfully from a massive infection in an unhealed surgical site or to starve myself, wither, and die in two or three weeks. He was saying it was time to give up. Time to die. Instead, he could have told us he felt he could not do a successful surgery and suggested we talk to someone else.

After I got out of the hospital, I felt as if I should say something to that doctor. I'm alive to write these words only because I didn't take his advice. I want him to see this book so he'll know how his call affected me and my family, and how he missed at least one opportunity to save a life.

Forever Changed

*The colostomy was like a dress rehearsal. That was about
as scared as I'd ever been. I was afraid of the surgery.
I was afraid I wasn't ever going to wake up.*

When we finally found a surgeon who would agree to do the
colostomy, I had the surgery immediately. Before the surgery, I
wrote a long letter to Matt, the letter I had wanted to write but
kept putting off. Then, just before they wheeled me into the oper-
ating room, I said goodbye to the people who were with me,
Craig, my mom, my mother-in-law, and my friend Sue. I gave
each person a hug and cried with them and whispered something
I wanted them to do. It was a life-advice thing: "If you want to
improve your life, you could do this." Afterwards, I felt embarrassed because I couldn't remember what I had said.

Once again, I had been assured by the anesthesiologist that
there would be little or no pain after surgery, but it was excruci-
ating. I was miserable and kept asking for more and more morphine all day. The nurse, Rachael—whom I will *never*
forget—kept telling me, "I can only give you this much. You have
to ask for another shot every half hour, and I will bring it to you,
but you have to wait half an hour between shots."

I said, "Look, I will be asking for it every half hour. Can you
just make a point to come every half hour with it, so I don't have
to call you?"

"No, you have to call me. You have to ask for it." This went on all day and into the night. I was uncomfortable in the bed, but I couldn't push myself into a comfortable position because any time I moved I had terrible pain. And I had to keep calling for Rachael. At ten or eleven o'clock I asked Rachael if she would call the doctor or the anesthesiologist. I said, "I need to get some sleep. I need a sleeping pill. And I need approval for more morphine."

It was clear she didn't want to call the doctor. She said, "I don't think they want you to sleep."

I said, "Why wouldn't they want me to sleep?"

About two o'clock in the morning, the anesthesiologist showed up in my room. I thought, "Good, Rachael finally called him." But he had been called in for an emergency and only had come up to see how I was doing. When he saw what pain I was in, he was aghast. He said, "I can't believe you've been going through this all day and all night." After the surgery, an epidural morphine drip had been set up to carry me until I could take oral painkillers. What we didn't know was that the epidural was never properly in place and never worked. The shots were all I was getting, and those were only supposed to be for extra pain. The anesthesiologist put me on an IV drip with the morphine and we were finally able to stabilize the pain.

What was important to me the first few days was dealing with pain, so I didn't have to deal with the colostomy. I couldn't even see it because of the dressing. I had no idea what it looked like, what it meant, what kinds of things I was going to have to do with it. I didn't care. I was glad to be alive, and I felt that everything was going to be okay if I could just get the pain under control. Finally, though, I had to confront the realities of the colostomy.

When they do a colostomy, they bring the colon to the surface of the skin so it sticks out on top of the abdomen. That's called the stoma, where the stool comes out. Mine began to work almost immediately, which is not always the case. I started passing gas, and every time I passed gas it would blow up the dressing. I called the nurse—Rachael, again—and said, "What am I going to do about this?" She poked a little hole in the bag with a pin and squeezed the air out.

A couple of nights later, I began to pass more than gas. It was a stool-smelling substance, very obnoxious. I woke up, and it had begun to leak out the little hole. The nurses must have poked the bag four or five times altogether, and this stuff had leaked out. It was all over my nightgown, all over me, all over my bed. I called for the nurse, and there was Rachael. I said, "We've got to get me cleaned up."

"Ohhh," she sighed. She helped me change my nightgown, and she kind of washed me off. She didn't change my sheets, just put another sheet and towel on top of what I had there, because I couldn't get out of bed. Rather than change my dressing, she placed gauze pads around the bag and taped them to my skin, leaving the hard work for the nurses to do the next day. And leaving me to smell it all night long.

I was so tired I just wanted to sleep, but the next morning I raised hell. I called the nurse manager and told her to keep Rachael away from me. She wrote the incident up in my chart, so the other nurses could read about it and know that this was not acceptable. Poking holes in the bag is not acceptable either; they should have changed the dressing. So I guess everybody got a little lesson out of that. But I didn't get anything out of it. There was no satisfaction for me. That was my introduction to the colostomy.

Usually, an enterostomal nurse comes to teach you about your colostomy and how to take care of your stoma. The nurse is scheduled to come three times: the first time to change your bandage and talk to you about it, the second time to change it with you, and the third time to have you do it while she watches, gives feedback and answers questions. Well, I healed so fast I was ready to go home from the hospital before I had my second and third lessons. The nurse came to my house and finished the last two lessons. But I think it should all be done in the hospital, so you can come home and start living with it, instead of coming home confused and uncertain and kind of afraid of it. I had millions of questions. I don't regret having had the operation. It saved my life. But nobody had told me what a colostomy actually was. What it meant.

You do find out what it is, and then you have to live with your body being forever changed and feeling ugly and uncomfortable because of it. My stoma is right on my waist, where a waistband would go and, unfortunately, that's the only place the surgeon could have put it. It was hard to wear pants and skirts afterward, and I didn't want it to show. My sister-in-law called from Hawaii and asked if I wanted some muumuus. I said, "Send them."

A System of Support

There's a very quick bond that grows between cancer patients—we just jump right in and get to know each other without any pretenses.

In June 1993, I began going to a support group, six women including myself, all with metastatic cancer. The group is my place for unloading. It feels comfortable. All someone has to do is say a few words and everybody joins in because we all understand what we're talking about. One woman said, "I'm having trouble talking to my friends about my illness. As soon as they see me, they say . . ." and all of us chimed in, "YOU LOOK SO GOOD!" We're all very aware that we take care of other people who are dealing with our illnesses.

Scientific research has shown that women with breast cancer who go to support meetings actually live longer than those who don't. I believe it's because we learn so much from each other— we learn about cancer, treatments, doctors, hospitals, and how to manage stress and communicate with friends and family—and we give each other the kind of support no one else can because of our in-depth understanding of what we're going through.

The group was formed by Ange Stephens, who facilitates our sessions. She had posted a flyer at Marin General Hospital for a group originally called "Women With Cancer." Nancy Lurmann saw the flyer and my friend Dorothy Geoghagen gave me Ange's name in the same week. Dorothy had belonged to a similar group in San Francisco. Nancy and I joined, and later one more person joined, so there were seven. Within months, two members died and one left because her cancer wasn't as serious as ours, and she needed something different.

In November 1993, I got a call from my E.T. (enterostomal) nurse. She said, "Linda, there's a young woman at Marin General who has just had a colostomy. She has colon cancer and it's metastasized to her liver. She has a lot of questions. Would you come over to talk to her?"

The doctors had suspected cancer but didn't know until they went in, and they didn't tell her anything until the surgery was over. She knew nothing about her disease, but she was scared to death. She asked me a stream of questions: "They found a few spots on my liver, but they'll go away, won't they? Chemotherapy will kill the cancer cells, won't it? Does chemo make you lose your hair? Will I get nauseous? I don't want to be nauseous."

I said, "You have a very long road ahead of you. I can't tell you exactly what is going to happen, but here is what you need to do to start. First, you need an oncologist." I told her what an oncologist does and gave her the names of mine and a few others. I said, "Ask your surgeon for a recommendation. To choose, use these criteria: one, good technical skills; two, good communication skills. Talk to at least two or three oncologists before you decide who you want.

"The next thing that will happen is that they will want to run a lot of tests."

She said, "You mean they're going to stick more needles in my arm? I have to drink some more yucky stuff?"

I said, "Yes, you're going to have to drink a lot more yucky stuff, you're going to have a lot more blood tests, you'll have to have a CT scan, and maybe an MRI [magnetic resonance imaging], so they can determine the extent of your disease. Then they will tell you whether you should have radiation or chemo or both, or even another surgery."

She was shocked. She asked, "Am I going to die?"

I realized that I had accepted this assignment without preparing myself for the tough questions. I couldn't believe that her doctor had told her so little; she didn't know *anything*. Why was *I* sent here to answer her questions?

Her family was just as naive. They assumed everything was all right because the surgery had been performed. But she was a very sick woman, and neither she nor her family had any idea that her chances of living even five years were very slim.

I wasn't going to be the one to tell her that she wasn't going to get well. I told her about my friends, Chris Jang and Jim Fuller, both of whom had had colon cancer that metastasized to the liver but were now in remission, working full time and carrying on with their normal activities.

She said, "What about you? Are you in remission?"

I said, "No. My cancer was too far advanced." She got big tears in her eyes and said, "Oh, my God, then you're . . ." I touched her hand and said it was okay. Meanwhile, I sent a prayer up to God to help me get through the discussion.

She asked, "Do you have a family?"

I said, "Yes, I have a husband and an eight-year-old child." She said, "How do you cope?" And I thought, "There's a question I can answer."

I said, "Day to day. One day I have an angry day, one day I cry all day, and then another day I'm cheerful like this. There are no easy answers to how you cope."

By now, she was sniffling and holding my hand. I said, "Let me tell you something. This is going to be very hard, and you can do it. There's nothing that's going to happen to you that you can't handle." I gave her my phone number and told her to call me. I gave her the name of my support group facilitator who had a group for people who've just been diagnosed. (This woman was not a candidate for the group I'm in—we sit around and talk about casket ornaments!)

She said, "I feel so close to you already."

I said, "There's a very quick bond that grows between cancer patients. We appreciate each other's strength and courage, and we're there for each other when needed." Then I left. I thought, "Doctors should be able to talk to their patients about what to expect once they've been diagnosed with cancer. This should not be the job of a volunteer."

In December 1993, I began to wonder if I was eligible for Hospice care. Hospice is a very special organization that works with terminally ill people. The doctor has to verify that you are terminally ill. There's no requirement that you have to be off all treatment.

The idea of Hospice here in Marin County, California, is to have care at home. I understand that in other places there might be a Hospice hospital. Here it's the concept that the patient should be allowed to die as comfortably as possible at home.

I called Hospice to ask about the qualifications. The woman I spoke with said, "Basically, your doctor needs to confirm that you have six months or less to live. That's the only requirement."

I said, "Unfortunately, I think I qualify."

She said, "We'll have to call your doctor." But she called back in a little while and said, "He wouldn't give us any information."

Then Dr. Spivack called and said, "I won't give Hospice information without talking to you first. Quite frankly, Linda, how many times have you been told that you had six months to live? If you want Hospice care, I'll tell them you have six months or less; no one reviewing your records would ever say that you have more than that, but you have shown a lot of people that doctors' predictions have little or nothing to do with a strong will to live." I backed off Hospice because I thought Dr. Spivack might be right. Psychologically, it might not be good for me to put myself in the six-month category.

In early January, however, I decided to go ahead. The Hospice people said, "We've had people on Hospice care for two years. Why not get the care if you're qualified?"

Hospice offers so many different services that I'm not sure I take advantage of all of them. I was assigned a nurse who, in my case, comes once a week for about two hours. She takes my vital signs and we talk about what's going on. She follows up with my doctor, and she also gives me any injection that I need.

My nurse, Michelle, decided in her forties to become a nurse, after she had worked as a Hospice volunteer. A Hospice nurse spoke to her volunteer group, and Michelle said, "That's what I want to do." She went back to school and got her credentials. Her career is being a Hospice nurse; she doesn't want to be any other kind of nurse.

The nurse develops a relationship with you. She's never said it, but I feel strongly that part of Michelle's role is to bond with me and be there for me as I die.

Hospice also has a counselor who comes as often as you want, not just for the patient, but for any family members or, I suppose, any caretakers who are with the patient on an ongoing basis. The counselor has worked with me, my mom, and my mother-in-law, and she'll work with Craig and Matt if they want help. She also runs support groups, including a post-death grief group for adults and another for children.

Hospice will send out home-care assistants to help you get up in the morning, make your bed, give you baths. After the colostomy, I used them five days a week to help with my baths. It was wonderful. Someone came at the same time every morning: "Wake up, let's get going, I'll get your bath." A volunteer would scrub my back, help me in and out of the bathtub. They treated me with such incredible respect that I didn't feel embarrassed about all the holes and bandages I've got hanging off my body. They were always rubbing lotion all over me and giving me massages. I remember thinking, "I should have done this when I was living my life, not living my death."

The Hospice volunteers help people out as needed. They'll drive you to doctor's appointments, go to the grocery store, run errands. If you are alone, or just want their help, people will come and stay with you around the clock so you always have somebody at your bedside. So you don't have to die alone. I've never seen a bill from Hospice.

Craig

〜

Everyone has specified roles. You're either the person who needs the care or you're the caregiver. As the caregiver, you focus on doing the best you can, on giving the best you can since it may be the last thing you can give. I focussed on controlling Linda's pain. On taking care of her physical needs. Her emotional needs. I was constantly trying to read the verbals and the nonverbals. Linda was reluctant to mention everything she needed because she felt as if she'd asked for so much already. So I was always watching, trying not to miss anything so I could give her the special care and love she needed.

Hospice, the hospital nursing staffs and the in-house nurses help you deal with the person's physical needs. Hospice counselors help with the emotional needs of both the cancer patient and the caregivers. I give Hospice so much credit. They deal with life and death situations every day. They have information about grieving, what's normal and what's abnormal, and it would have been helpful for me to have taken more advantage of their services.

Religion is a good handhold for a lot of people, although Hospice says it's normal to be angry at God. It's a double-edged sword: "If God can do everything, then why did He let this happen?" That's why counseling, regardless of religion or other philosophical beliefs, is good. Because it will help if you say, "Okay, I'm not going to be cast into Hell or wherever just because I hate God for a short time." Commonweal in Bolinas, California, also has some ways of alerting you to the fact that as a caregiver you have as much healing to do as the cancer patient.

My mother-in-law talked to the Hospice counselors. At the time, I thought, "Oh, no, I'm fine. I'm not the person who is dying. I'm the person who is trying to help the person get through dying." I didn't even imagine that counseling was a significant need of mine.

I would definitely encourage people who are helping a loved one go through a similar situation to watch out for themselves. You need to understand what you are going to lose. You need to take care of yourself and anticipate what's going to happen. If you haven't taken care of your own needs, what's going to happen to you when your loved one dies?

When Someone You Know Has Cancer . . .

*If I were to give advice to people who want to know
what to say to someone with cancer, I'd say,
"Don't have the first thing you ask be all the symptoms."*

It's difficult to understand what it's like to have cancer unless you or someone close to you has it. I couldn't understand what it was like to have a family member with cancer until my dad was diagnosed and I realized that I was at a loss as to what to say or do.

Four months after my cancer was diagnosed, our friend Chris Jang, who is ten years younger than I am, also had surgery for colon cancer. I was the first person he called when he went into the hospital. When he told me, I had the same feeling that any other person would have had: "My God, what do I say?"

It's never easy to know how to respond to this kind of news, but there are some things that don't work well with me. For instance, if people start asking questions right away—"How did you know you had it?" "Where did it hurt?"—it sounds as if they are mostly concerned about whether they might have it, too. And I don't like to hear stories about other people who have cancer and now are all right. I don't need people trying to cheer me up. I appreciate good intentions, but I want to say, "Wait a minute. This isn't your friend Ethel's cancer, it isn't your Uncle Henry's cancer, it's my cancer, and I'm going to have it the way I have it, and it doesn't help to compare it to anybody else's.

As far as I'm concerned, Paul Tsongas said it all during a TV interview with Jane Pauley. He didn't look well, but he was still swimming and running. Still fighting his cancer. She asked whether he felt remorse for not having disclosed his physical condition when he was running for the presidential nomination. He said, "But I did disclose it fully. Some publications chose to print the disclosure, and some did not." Then he said that at one of his public appearances during the primary, somebody started telling him he had no right to run for office when he had cancer. Tsongas immediately interrupted, pointed his finger at the guy, and said, "Listen, don't you lecture to me about cancer. Until you get cancer and you deal with cancer, you don't know anything about it." I was sitting there saying, "YES!"

I know sometimes people think if they don't mention it, I'll be more comfortable. Well, I'm not. I'm more uncomfortable if it's not mentioned. It's on my mind a lot of the time. I'm sure it's on other people's minds too.

My family has been so busy being strong for me. Craig told me that after the first surgery they wiped off their tears when they knew I was returning from the recovery room because they didn't want me to see them crying. They didn't want to upset me. Well, I was already upset. They couldn't upset me any more.

Some people think that a more positive attitude is all I need. Be sparkling and vibrant and courageous. During the first few months, I liked to shock people like that. I wanted them to know that I didn't have much time, so we could really talk, say what was on our minds, deal more honestly. I said to a relative who I love dearly, "They only gave me a fifty percent chance of living for one year."

She replied, "I'm going to send you a book about somebody who had incurable cancer and she's miraculously fine now."

I asked, "What kind of cancer did she have?"

"Breast."

"I don't have breast cancer, I have colon cancer and it's spread all the way through my abdomen, and I have to face the facts and prepare myself for a shorter life span." I gave her a half-hour lecture about the fact that some people do go into remission, and some doctors do make mistakes, but my chances are slim. Afterward I realized that instead of lecturing her on statistics, I should have just told her that I need her help, care, and concern, not a pep talk.

Some people think that if I read a certain book or try a new herbal tea or whatever, things will turn out differently. It makes me want to invite them to spend a day or a week with me and see what I do to stay healthy. Go with me to one or two doctor appointments, watch me get hooked up to a chemo pump, get a CT scan, get a blood test, get an injection, have an enema, force down my food, consume special high-calorie drinks, go to a support group meeting, get a massage, take vitamins, call 1-800-4-CANCER to research a new drug, take a nap, meditate, practice yoga, etc., etc., etc.

What I'd like people to remember is that when I'm feeling down, I don't like to be told, "Cheer up, things are going to get better." It would be more helpful to ask me questions such as, "What are you thinking about? Are you worried? Do you want to talk about it? Is there any way I can help?" Questions like that are far more helpful than saying, "You should be meditating, you should be drinking a certain tea, you should be taking beta carotene, you should see this doctor in Mexico, you should be visualizing your cancer cells."

Relationships become so dynamic when one person is extremely ill. I've found it very interesting to see who stayed close and who drifted away. A support group friend, Lori Fisher, put it this way:

> Our values and perceptions change overnight. We begin to look at the world differently, and our priorities flip-flop. We start behaving differently. Friends and family members notice that we've changed and have difficulty understanding what is going on. In some cases, they resist our changes because the roles in the relationship begin to be redefined.

I think that few people are able to see clearly what is going on, to analyze it:

> Why is my best friend now not my best friend? Oh, I see, I'm suddenly expecting something of my friends that I never expected before. I'm making demands, or I'm assuming they are going to provide something I need when they've never provided it before. It was never part of the contract.

For example, suddenly I expect a friend to be nurturing who's never been nurturing before. I'm asking for something I need that that person is not used to giving and not comfortable giving. As friends, we will continue to care about each other, but we don't seem as compatible as before, and that friend moves out of the spotlight because now I need people who are nurturing.

If a relationship was originally based on doing things together, going places, seeking adventures and fun, it now seems boring. I haven't seen a movie in a theater or eaten out for months. All I can do is listen and ask questions. Our conversation drifts while we seek topics of interest to both of us. And then we find ourselves wondering why our relationship is disintegrating.

I know we get different things from different relationships. It's a matter of realizing why some people come more into focus while others drop back. I have to understand why I'm feeling irritated with somebody. For instance, I expected a compassionate, sympathetic, nurturing, helpful response from one friend but didn't receive it. In fact, she would come up with elaborate excuses for not coming to visit me. I was becoming more and more irritated with her because she didn't seem to care. She would call and say, "You sound really good." It didn't matter how

I felt. So I have an enlarged tumor, a great deal of inflammation, the worst pain I've ever had in my life—she would still say, "You sound great. You must be better."

Finally, I told her, "How I sound has nothing to do with how I feel. I'm very sick, I'm getting sicker, and I don't want you to tell me how I feel. I'll tell you how I feel." It was shocking for her. She didn't respond at all except at the end of the phone conversation she said, "Well, I'll call you tomorrow and see how you're doing . . . Oh. I'll call you tomorrow to say hello." The odd thing was that I was perfectly willing to let go of that relationship. I no longer had time for it. I would regret it if we never spoke again, but I won't regret it if she's not around. I realize that she's not capable of or interested in providing what I need right now.

Fortunately, some relationships blossom and grow during times like this. I received a visit from another friend I had known for years but hadn't been close to, mainly because we hadn't devoted enough time to our relationship. We chatted for a while, and then he brought up the topic of his spirituality. He said he doesn't talk about it much but he wondered if I would be interested. I was flabbergasted to learn of his interest in that area, and we talked about it for nearly two hours. It was the most stimulating visit I'd had in a long time. Something tells me we'll be talking more and that he will be a comfort to me on the remainder of my journey.

Carolyn

(Linda's friend and business associate)

❧

Whenever someone we're close to dies, we learn more about life and death and about ourselves. About how we deal with things. How we make choices. What we're afraid of. And even what's important.

When Linda died I lost the person I was most used to talking with about new things I learned. She would have been the best one to talk with about what it was like to be dead. But we'll never be able to talk about that—or anything—ever again.

Going through Linda's cancer and dying was an "in-real-time" (as Linda would say) learning experience for me. Talking to her about what she was going through. Doing our last workshop together. Seeing her officially shut down the business. I was torn about having new business cards made that didn't say "Linda Mukai and Associates." I loved being Linda's associate, and my new cards were proof that we wouldn't be working together again. I was scared to leave town during her last few weeks, afraid I'd miss seeing her for the last time or be gone when she died and not know for days.

I admired Linda deeply, totally; I marvelled at her from the first time I knew of her to the end of her life. I felt lucky, lucky, lucky to share some space with her. All my family and most of my friends and colleagues knew about her and her cancer. Now I find when I talk about Linda's illness I tend to say many of the same things I heard from her and learned. For example, Linda introduced me to the difference between healing and curing. She knew she wasn't going to be cured. She focussed on being healed. But if friends sent "cures" like herbal teas, quartz crystals, or rituals to follow, she accepted them.

Maybe it was her customer service mind-set, but she always seemed to know who could deal with what and who would talk about what. But it didn't seem fair to me that she worked so hard on making her friends comfortable. I thought we should be focussing on her needs instead.

In one conversation, we talked about humor. Linda had lots of funny things to say about being sick and about dying. I was glad when she told me she knew she could always share her black humor with me. That she knew I'd listen and join in. That I could make her laugh and I'd laugh with her. She said she needed that outlet and not everyone likes to hear jokes about cancer and death. Too bad for them.

I miss Linda terribly. Now when I read about people or companies or events I know she'd be interested in I catch myself thinking, "Oh, that's a good one. I'll have to tell Linda about that." I wonder when I'll stop doing this. Sometimes, though, I think she hears me, especially if it's a really good one. And besides, being Linda, she'll be there if that's what I need. That's Linda.

Janis

It's July 1994. As we have done since we began this book, Linda
and I hold our meetings in her bedroom, a large, cluttered room
that looks out on her newly landscaped back yard complete with
a basketball court and a fish pond spanned by a red wooden
bridge. There are several large plants, an upholstered chaise
lounge, a soft pale carpet. Books and medicines and glasses of
water and magazines cover the night stands and the bed, and
videotapes are piled on the shelf below the television. I step over
cardboard boxes half filled with things she wants to save for Matt
and pull the large wicker chair close to the bed so we can talk. The
bed has huge pillows. The colors are mostly grey and cream, soft
and warm. There is what I think is a Frida Kahlo print on the wall,
a large dark-skinned woman in bright colors. The stuffed elephant that used to sit next to the patio door now lives in Matt's
room. There is a gas fireplace, but I've never seen it lit. Linda
spends most of her time in this room now, although she always
tries to get up, shower, dress, and put on makeup before settling
back down on the bed or the chaise.

Linda has less time now. She can see no farther ahead than a
day, an hour, even a few minutes. "When I put my head down for
a nap," she tells me, "I know there's a good chance I won't wake
up." She does not expect to be around for Thanksgiving or
Christmas this year; she might not make it until Matt's first day of

fourth grade. Dottie, March, and Craig say the same: "We're taking it one day at a time."

As Linda's time grows shorter, her need to finish this book becomes more urgent. Yesterday she faxed me a new introduction to review. I phoned to say that it arrived and added, "I'll probably get to it over the weekend." I could hear the disappointment in her silence. What she really wanted—but wouldn't say she wanted—was for me to review it right away and tell her what I thought. She couldn't be sure about the weekend.

I often feel that I'm disappointing Linda these days. I do not share her sense of urgency. I understand it, but I do not feel it. When I'm busy, and I usually am busy, I find it hard to make the book my first priority. I have to keep reminding myself that Linda has an entirely different sense of time. I feel ashamed when I realize that when Linda dies, my first or even my third reaction might be relief: no more pressure to keep the book moving forward, to get it done before it's too late. I try not to feel guilty. But I don't think you can help feeling that way sometimes when you're close to someone who is seriously ill. You can't help disappointing them. You can't help feeling irritated and impatient. You can't make the bad feelings go away, and it doesn't help to keep beating yourself because you have them. But they're not nice feelings. Not nice at all.

One reason I keep losing the sense of urgency is that I still find it hard to think of Linda as a dying person. She still projects such vitality. She is still so *alive*. She doesn't really seem connected to her body, which is little more than skin and bones. The person is so much *there*, even when the body tenses with pain, even as the body shifts and turns in a futile attempt to find a comfortable resting position. Even though there is a tumor growing out of her navel and a shunt sticking out of her arm, even though she is in more or less constant pain, Linda is still able to laugh, a little. Still able to work furiously on the book, and organize her household, and worry about Matt.

As the warm summer days drift by, it becomes more and more evident that Linda is losing her battle to stay alive. Her body is betraying her, and she is forced to watch. In August, I visit her in the hospital where she is hooked up to tubes that feed blood and nutrients and medicines into her body. A bag collects her urine. A bag collects her stool. Her legs and feet are so swollen that they seem to belong not to Linda but to a stout elderly woman who has neglected her health. She is bleeding internally. She has obstructions in her kidneys. Tumors are growing throughout her abdominal cavity. Yet she continues to fight. "I've been waiting for the time to come when I will be ready to let go," she says grimly, "but now I don't think that time is ever going to come." I know that when she is feeling very, very sick, when she is in great pain and exhausted, she wishes she would fall asleep and not wake up. But it is a momentary wish. Give her a moment of energy, a moment free of pain, a moment where the drugs have not overwhelmed her senses, and she desperately wants to live. She says she will fight right up until the last, and I believe her. That is who she is.

I think about how *I* feel. I feel sad. Angry. Frustrated that there is nothing I can do to help. A little bored with it all, and angry with myself for feeling bored. I remind myself that I don't have to feel. I only have to observe. Fat chance. Out the window I see blue skies and green trees. A beautiful summer day. I'm not sure what I'm doing with my life, but I know it's not enough.

I realize that dying, especially the way Linda is dying, is about losing control. Linda has lost control of her body, of her ability to prolong her life through the sheer force of her will. Craig and March and Dottie have lost control; they can do nothing to prolong Linda's life or even make her "comfortable." When my friend Diane's uncle's lifelong companion was in the hospital dying, her uncle raged at the doctors and the hospital staff because they could not make his friend comfortable. Couldn't keep his friend alive. I understand. It's infuriating that no one can soothe the person's pain, heal the person's body, keep the person going. Doctors and nurses should be able to do something, you think, if only they would pay attention. After all, they're the ones who know. They're the ones with the magic.

Linda comes home, but a few weeks later they will take her back to the hospital in an ambulance, not to die, but to have her kidney stent replaced because it is backing up, and a backup would kill her. Everyone agrees that Linda is dying. For the past week she has been able to do nothing but lie in the hospital bed that has replaced the chaise lounge in her bedroom. Her arms are so thin I can see the outline of bone beneath the skin; her legs and toes are so swollen from fluid retention that they seem about to burst. She is connected to a book-sized contraption that allows her morphine on demand—the dream of every addict. Except it's not a dream and Linda's not an addict. Despite the morphine, she can never get comfortable. She falls asleep in the middle of a sentence, then wakes up a minute or two later searching for the words to complete the thought. Everyone waits. Matt comes into her room and touches her hair, then leaves. He insists on being present when her bandage is changed, even though it's past his bedtime, and Linda lets him stay. Dottie leaves sodden tissues on the coffee table after her sessions with the Hospice counselor. March's eyes are red as she explains how much she has learned from Linda, how honored she is to be here. Craig moves slowly, carefully, his eyes distant; there is a new streak of grey in his hair.

Their house is beautiful. There's a new fountain in the entry hall. The fountain is beautiful. Linda refuses to let go. At a safe distance from the day-to-day dying, I am still exhausted by it. Dottie's voice on my answering machine tells me that they got Linda home from the hospital and the stent replacement went well. I think that "well" is a relative term. The procedure bought another few hours, another few days, perhaps a week or more, of half-life, of pain, of discomfort. I love Linda and want her to live. I even understand her refusal to let go, but I wish she could, for her sake, and for the sake of her family. God forbid I should ever have to make such a decision, whether to die now or die later. And who am I to judge Linda's decision? She has an enormously strong life force, and it is firmly rooted in this world.

LETTING GO

Making Preparations, Just in Case

I expect to be buried with my To Do list in my hand and a little saying on my marker, "She Never Finished Her To Do list."

Audrey Hepburn's death in January 1993 scared me. I had just read she had colon cancer, and two months later she was gone. I wanted to know, could I suddenly die? Could things suddenly turn for the worse and the time run out?

In June 1993, I felt as if I were going into the second year of illness the way I went into the first year: it was still hard to believe that I was going to die. I was feeling so strong. But I was also afraid of having the tables turned very quickly. I felt as if I still had things to accomplish.

Craig and I have closure every day. But my To Do list keeps growing. In the middle of the night I do mental pirouettes: "Take another look at the will and the Durable Power of Attorney"; "Decide about my remains." I have no idea how I want to be disposed of yet. When I saw the radiation oncologist in August, I realized that I'd known I was under risk for a year and a half and still hadn't decided whether I wanted to be buried or cremated. I want to make that decision, or at least discuss it with Craig.

I want to burn a stack of old correspondence, poems I wrote back in college, journals, things no one else needs to know about.

I had planned to build a fire one cold day when nobody else was home, read it all, and toss it in. But I decided I'd better not wait for the cold season. Craig said, "I'll tell you what. We'll light a fire one night, even though it's August. You can read me the ones you like and then we'll toss 'em in the fire, roast a few marshmallows."

Then there are the things I want to give away. It would be fun to make boxes of stuff for friends and family members. Somebody might like to have my professional materials, someone else my clothes. Craig and I have talked about making a video, "A day in the life of our family." I make up voices for Matt's stuffed animals, and Craig wants me to act out some of those characters on the tape. He also wants to have a family picture taken, since we don't have a good, recent picture of the three of us.

Matt and I have grown closer. He is an incredible little human being. He's smart and cute and funny and clever. He's amazingly curious about the world. He's very nurturing, and I depend upon him for a lot of my emotional care. I can cry in front of him. He holds me, he pats my head, he helps me walk down the hall when I'm having trouble walking, he jumps in bed and cuddles with me when I'm hurting. I think it's good for him to have the opportunity to give to me. I hope he'll remember that he was helpful to me. I don't know what he's thinking—sometimes he won't talk about it—but I know he worries and is scared. I hope his doctor is helping him.

I wrote him some letters, which Craig will give him at the right times in his life. One is a letter I wrote when I was in the hospital the night before the colostomy, when I thought I might not survive the surgery. I read it over a few weeks later and didn't change a word. Basically it's two letters. The first one is about our decision to adopt him. I wanted him to know that we always loved him and always wanted him, even before he was born. The second letter tells him goodbye. It tells him that he doesn't need to feel guilty that I was ill and died. It also says that I didn't want to die, but life isn't always fair. And I thank him for all the love and nurturing he gave me while I was sick.

I also wrote a letter I want Craig to give him when he is eleven or twelve. It's about how tough it is to be an adolescent. I talk about my own difficult experiences at that age.

I've been working on a scrapbook for him, to tell my story, what kind of a kid I was, who I am. The book is a little writing with a lot of pictures and clippings. When I started, I thought, "I can't remember anything from those early years." But once I got into it, I found I remembered a lot. It became important that I tell the truth about my childhood. I want Matt to understand why I turned out the way I did. So I'm trying to paint a picture of what my home was like and what school was like and who was important and what hurt and what didn't bother me.

I put together a trunk of things I want Matt to have. I've saved things for him since his birth: his first tiny Pampers, a few little outfits, an album of pictures and information about his birth mother, a few other personal items.

A couple of years ago I bought the *Life* magazines from the weeks Craig and I were born. I have some articles about significant events during Matt's lifetime. I'm putting things away that might not matter to him until he's in his twenties or thirties or even beyond that.

I realize there is a "letting go" process going on. I need to tie up the loose ends of my life before I move on to accepting and preparing for my death. I wish I had done these things earlier, when I had more strength and energy.

One night I told Craig, "Honey, if I don't wake up one of these mornings, the bottom drawer of my night table has everything you need in it."

He said, "Like what?"

I opened the drawer and showed him a stack of white envelopes. I said, "Here's a file for you. It has financial information, letters to friends and family, letters to Matt." Another envelope is labeled, "To Craig regarding services, et cetera." Inside it says, "Here are my wishes regarding funeral services," and there are notes about who should perform the service, where it should be, charities I favor, what kind of service I would prefer to have. The notes say things like, "Keep costs to a minimum; don't spend too much money on a box." It has notes about music I like that he might consider for the service. I named two or three people I would like to speak. I tell him, "I'll leave the rest to you, Mom, and my pastor." I don't want to make all the decisions.

In one of the envelopes are some booklets about talking with children about death. I've collected financial information I was afraid Craig would forget. For example, I included information about my benefits under my retirement plan from an old employer. On the day I would have turned fifty-five, Craig will become eligible for a pension from them. Isn't that nice for him?

One envelope contains a letter to family and friends to be opened at my death and read at my funeral or memorial service. I had started writing something to be read at my funeral, a few words to Craig, a few words to Mom, and a few words to Matt. Then I thought I'd better say a few words to my dad and my step-mother. And my mother-in-law and father-in-law, who have been awfully good to me. And my sister Susan's been wonderful, and there are a few friends I'd better mention. About halfway through, I thought, "Well, now I know why nobody does this. You can't stop." I wrapped it up quickly, and then I said goodbye.

All this, the white envelopes, the letters, make me feel that I'm ticking off the unfinished business, that I'm still in control. It's like saying, "I may be dead, but I still have a voice in the disposal of my remains and how my goodbyes are said."

Shopping for Cemeteries

I don't know what I want at the end.
I don't even know what I want now.

Part of my unfinished business was deciding how I wanted to be disposed of and what kind of service I preferred. I wanted to make those decisions while I was feeling well. While they weren't so frightening and painful. So one day Nancy Lurmann, my friend who also has metastasized colon cancer, and I took a field trip to see mortuaries and cemeteries. We thought we could relieve our families of some of those difficult tasks.

This field trip was not something we wanted to do with our husbands, friends, or other family members. We felt as if nobody else would be able to handle it. Certainly, nobody else would understand our morbid curiosity, our laughter, and our tears.

We jumped in the car laughing and thinking, "Do we really, really, really want to do this?" At the first mortuary, an odor overwhelmed us as soon as we stepped inside the door. It was a stale old carpet and furniture smell, and we knew right away that it was not a place where we wanted our family and friends to have to come. The interior was dark and dingy, and the furnishings were covered in shiny, worn green velour. We left quickly, knowing we could tell our spouses, "Don't go there because you won't like it."

At the next mortuary we were met by a secretary who introduced us to what I would call a salesman, although his title might have been "advisor" or "counselor." He was very helpful. We asked a lot of questions and he gave us a lot of information. He stressed the importance of allowing close family members, especially children, to view the body. Earlier my mother had said, "I'm going to view your body, so you may as well get used to it, because that's how I'm going to say goodbye." So I had already planned that immediate family members who wanted to, could, but the casket was going to be closed at the services. We asked why viewing the body was important.

He said, "It's a time-honored tradition because it speeds the grieving process along. It makes it true for people that the person is dead, that he or she has left that body. That the thing in the casket is not alive. Even if people are present for your death, even if they are holding your hand while you leave your body, it is still important for them to be able to see that the body has been prepared for burial and that's it—the person is gone. They can say, 'That's just a dead body. It's not Linda. She's gone and at peace.' It's part of the separation."

Nancy had told the salesman why we had come, that we both had cancer and wanted to do as much of this for our families as we could. At first he felt a little uncomfortable. Then he grinned and said, "This is an extremely courageous thing you're doing." I'll give you some paperwork to fill out that will make it easier on your family. But it's important to leave a lot of decision-making to them because that's part of their grieving process, too. It also gives them something to do. Sitting around crying, having people in, is very difficult. A way to escape is taking care of the business of the disposition." Nancy was hilarious—she asked me, "Are we going to leave the last furniture-buying decision to our spouses when we've always picked out our own furniture?" She was referring to the caskets, which we would see later.

We asked about the pros and cons of burial versus cremation. He said, "Sixty percent of Marin County people now are choosing cremation, but I would only recommend it if every person in your family is completely comfortable with it. Let's face it, it's fire, no matter what kinds of other spiritual things you might attach to it, and there's nothing romantic about fire. We scrape up the ashes—there isn't that much left—and put them in a cardboard box until somebody decides what to do with them. You can decide to put them in an icebox, put them in an urn, scatter them, whatever, but basically what you have is a burned body. If that's what your family feels comfortable with, if they like the spiritual aspects of that, then do it. But if anybody feels uncomfortable with it, it will be a nightmare for them to picture it, think about it, dream about it and so forth.

"You might want to give burial a second thought. The thing about burial is that people can say, 'That's where her bones are,' even if they never visit the grave site again. If they want to, they can go there, take some flowers and have a discussion with those bones."

I asked, "Do people actually visit graves? I think I might do it a time or two, but I don't know how long I would keep up something like that."

He said, "That's the tendency. People have a few last things they have to say, or they may have some kind of annual ritual on an anniversary or a birthday or something. They might want to go there, take care of the grave, meditate, pray."

After our discussion, we asked to view the chapel. He said, "Sure, but I want to warn you that both of our chapels currently have open caskets with corpses in them." Nancy had never seen a dead person in her life. She said, "Linda, I feel like I need to see a dead person. Would you go up there with me?"

So I walked up to the front of a chapel with her. We didn't get terribly close, but she was at least able to see that it did not look at all like a living person. She said she had this sense that the hand moved or something and I said, "Yeah, I get the sense that the chest is going up and down." But we both knew that the poor man was no longer residing in that body.

The salesman told us that here in California, with our "Type A" lifestyles, people tend not to attend funerals. Even when they do, the body isn't usually shown, and people usually don't have time, or the desire, to go to the cemetery. He thinks the result is that people are becoming more and more fearful of death because they haven't been exposed to it. He said that you get desensitized to it if you go to funerals.

I remembered that when I was a child in Oklahoma, when one of my stepfather's coworkers had a death in his family, everyone from the office would go to the funeral. Sometimes Mom and I would go too, even though we may not have known the family, to pay our respects. The casket was always open, and everyone approached the body to say good-by. We would go to the cemetery afterwards, and then bring food to the family's home. I saw quite a few dead bodies when I was a kid. I still don't like looking at them; I don't think you ever get used to it.

The salesman took us upstairs to look at caskets, and he talked about whether they were airtight and leakage-proof. There are so many decisions to make. I can see why families end up spending a lot of money, because when you're bereaved all you think about is getting the best for the person you love, and of preserving the body. But let's face it—that body is *not* going to be preserved. Your skeleton may survive for a while, but the rest of you is going to be gone in short order. I thought it was important to tell Craig, "Think about this key fact: I'm going to be gone. Pick a box you feel happy with, put my body in there, and bury it. Don't spend the family fortune on the trimmings."

As we left the mortuary, Nancy and I found ourselves laughing uncontrollably. Nancy asked, "Do you think that guy was trying to sell us on burial over cremation because the fee is larger?" I said, "Do you think he works on commission?"

Next, we went to a cemetery that had a mortuary attached. The salesman took us to the chapel and for a ride around the cemetery in his car. We felt that although the cemetery was somewhat pastoral, sort of Marin-rustic, it was unkempt, messy, and shabby. The tombstones leaned in different directions, and the grass was brown from lack of water. In areas where they were clearing more space, there were fallen trees and brush that hadn't been picked up in a long time.

The man told us the name for each area, "The Oaks" (not only were there no oaks, there weren't any trees at all) and "The Redwoods" (again, no trees). "We only have a few plots left here.

There's a couple of spots left over there. All the plots in this area have been sold. The people haven't died yet, but they're all presold."

The so-called chapel was actually a hallway surrounded by crypts. We were again assaulted by one of those smells you never want to smell again. I wondered, Is it the bodies or is it just plain old dank uncirculated air? "Where do you seat all the people?" I asked.

He said, "We set up chairs going all the way through the mausoleum."

I thought, "No way!" It would be gruesome. It would give people nightmares.

We told this salesman the same thing we told the first one, that we were friends with metastatic cancer and less than a year to live, that we wanted to make some decisions about our funeral and burial arrangements so we could spare our families the trouble. But this man misunderstood our relationship. Halfway along the tour, he began to talk about double plots, double niches. Nancy and I looked at each other, and we realized that he thought we were lesbians. He said, "It's such a coincidence that you both have cancer at the same time. What a tragedy." We were practically splitting our sides trying not to laugh, but neither of us corrected him. It really didn't matter what he thought, and he was trying so hard to be nice. He was so proud of his cemetery that when he tried to close the sale, we couldn't bear to hurt his feelings. We told him we'd have to discuss it with our families.

There are other cemeteries in Marin and in Colma, south of San Francisco. Supposedly there are more dead people than alive in Colma. Nancy and I decided Colma would be our next field trip, but we never took it. She decided to be buried there, and I haven't decided yet.

We also discussed the fact that our husbands may remarry, and they might be buried next to someone else. So our bodies might be buried alone, with no family members near us at all.

It was much harder to go on this field trip than I thought it would be. My throat was sore from fighting the tears. I kept thinking, "I'm really going to die—this is no joke." I hated the whole idea of my body going to a mortuary, to be handled by strangers. I thought it's too bad that when you die you don't just dissolve, or be . . . beamed up.

Thinking about all of this made me even more nervous about my illness. It made me want to put off the inevitable as long as possible. I thought, Why am I having to do this? This isn't fair. Why couldn't I wait until I'm ninety-five years old, let Matt make these decisions for me when I'm in some nursing home and don't know the difference." But I guess that's not to be.

On the way home, Nancy and I were both afraid that although we made it through the day, we wouldn't be able to make it through the night. I didn't have any trouble going to sleep that night, but I did wake up from a very bad dream with my heart pounding. Somebody was chasing me, and I was trying to dart in and out of the windows of a house. I was crawling under beds and pushing furniture aside, trying to get away from someone, but he was always within arm's reach. I was screaming in the dream, and I woke up aware that my heart was beating harder than it had ever beat before. I woke Craig. "Honey, honey, honey, wake up, wake up, my heart's beating really hard."

Craig jumped up and took my pulse. I remember him saying, "Honey, you're just having a dream," and it seemed like my pulse slowed, so I don't know if my heart was ever beating that hard or if I was dreaming that it was. He patted me and cuddled me and I went back to sleep. I didn't have any more dreams like that for the rest of the night.

Learning from a Loss

❦

*My friend's death taught me that everyone involved with me
not only needs to know what my wishes are, but to have some
level of knowledge about what can happen—what to look for,
how to respond, what to do. Not only intimate friends and family,
but even the people who volunteer to drive me to the doctor.*

On January 7, 1994, my dear friend Nancy Lurmann died. She
had become such an important part of my life. We had parallel
diseases, metastatic colon cancer diagnosed within three months
of one another, and parallel life situations. We and our children
were close in age; we had happy marriages of about the same
length; we went to the same oncologist and had consulted with
the same two others; we had the same insurance company; we
lived within a block of one another. There were so many parallels
that there was always this question in the back of our minds: Who
would go first?

We both assumed I would be the first because we thought I
was in worse shape, and most of the time I was. My disease was
seen as metastatic from the time of my first surgery, and hers
didn't appear to be. A year after her surgery she had a recurrence
of cancer, while on chemo. Two huge tumors had grown, one the
size of a tennis ball, and she had to have a hysterectomy. I'd
already had a hysterectomy in 1988, because of fibroid tumors.

But shortly after my colostomy, Nancy also had a blockage, a second one. Her cancer had spread more than the doctors had thought, and because of the location of the tumors, it was necessary to do an ileostomy. Also, she had a more aggressively growing cell than I had.

The worst of it for Nancy was that her pain could not be alleviated. She was taking MS Contin, the same time-released morphine tablets I was on, but it wasn't enough. The Pain Control Team at her hospital did a pain blockage procedure, injecting alcohol in a sac of nerves in her back, to numb the abdomen and pelvis. Two days later, she was screaming in pain again.

Right before Christmas, Nancy told me she was going back into the hospital for another procedure, to sever some nerves in her spine. I said, "Gee, Nancy, will you be able to walk?" She laughed and said, "You know, I didn't even ask that question. I'm at the point where I don't even care." She was so drugged that she wasn't herself a lot of the time. She'd stumble over her words, and she couldn't remember what she was saying. I'd say, "Why are they doing this procedure?" and she wouldn't be able to explain it.

They decided not to sever the nerves after all. Instead, they put in an epidural continuous drip of morphine. A few days later, on a Thursday, her friend and her mother were driving her to the University of California Medical Center in San Francisco to have the epidural checked because they thought it was leaking, when Nancy began to have convulsions. Her friend and her mother didn't know how to get to the hospital, so they pulled off the road and called the paramedics, who tried to revive her.

She continued to convulse for two hours. The epidural had become infected, and Nancy had spinal meningitis. She went into a coma. She was put in the intensive care unit and connected to life support equipment.

As soon as Dr. Spivack learned about this, he asked that she be taken off the machines. He knew Nancy had made out a Durable Power of Attorney for Health Care in which she had clearly stated that she did *not* want to be put on life support, but there wasn't a copy available when she was admitted. Nancy's husband, Fred, brought the document to the hospital but still could not convince the hospital administrators to remove the life support. The hospital attorneys and ethics board became involved.

Friday morning I had an appointment with Dr. Spivack, so I went to the U.C. Medical Center early to see Nancy first. All Thursday night Nancy had been appearing in my dreams, asking "What should I do, stay or go?" Whether it was Nancy asking for my help or me grappling with what I would do in her situation, the voice continued throughout the night, discussing the benefits and drawbacks of staying and going.

A neurologist was with her when I got to the hospital, going over his checklist one last time. I talked with her family, and then I went across the street for my appointment with Dr. Spivack, who said, "Things over there are going to be rectified very quickly." I practically ran back to the hospital.

Nancy was still in a coma, but her eyes were open. I felt her presence, although she was unable to communicate. The life support already had been removed, and she was in her last moments, but I didn't realize that.

It was shocking to see her. She had gained twenty or thirty pounds, just in fluid, in the past week. Fred warned me and Ann Nathan, another cancer support group member, not to go in because he knew it would be very hard on us to see her that way. And it really was. When I got home, I got out all the photographs I had of her so I could remember how she really looked.

Fred left Ann and me in the room with Nancy. She took two or three more breaths while we were talking to her and holding her hands, and then she was gone. I don't know if she had been waiting for us, but Ann and I had felt we had to see her. We had to say goodbye.

All the support group members went to Nancy's funeral service at Sinai Memorial Chapel in San Francisco. The chapel was full. Fred did the eulogy himself, and he did it with such tender love and affection. He said it was his gift to Nancy. He wanted us to know what a wonderful person she was and how much he'd loved her. It was a great tribute to her that so many people came to the service when she'd only lived in the Bay Area for four years.

Nancy's father also spoke, and then the rabbi had Nancy's daughter, Kaitlin, come up to the front. He asked Kaitlin, "Where in your body are you going to remember your mom?" She said, "Here and here," pointing to her head and her heart. He said, "Let's count in Hebrew the things that you learned from your mom." He went through seven things that Kaitlin had learned from her mother. He said, "Why do you think we picked seven?" She said, "Because I'm seven years old?" and he said, "Yes. Every year for the rest of your life, I bet you'll be able to list one more thing that you learned from your mom. Those are all gifts she left to you, and no one can ever take them away. No matter what happens, she will always be your mommy and you can always remember her and love her."

It was so sweet. Kaitlin smiled, and she cried a little and she laughed a little. It was clear that Fred and Nancy had designed the service with her in mind.

While the family went to the private burial, our support group members came back to my house. We were able to relax and have lunch before going over to Nancy's house to visit with her family. Craig and Mom missed the funeral service, but they joined us to talk about Nancy and grieve and laugh and remember.

Nancy's death was another communication lesson. I asked Dr. Spivack, "How do I avoid what happened to her?"

He said, "You've got to carry that Durable Power of Attorney for Health Care on your person. Keep copies of it in your car. I need a copy, the hospital should have a copy. Keep copies of it everywhere." He told me that if I did go into a coma at home, my family shouldn't call 911, because the paramedics' job is to revive people. They should call Hospice. Or call him or Dr. Oppenheim.

I learned a lot from Nancy's experience. One thing I've done is to make a telephone tree. That way, friends who want to know how I'm doing can call another person for information and then, once they know, can decide whether or not to call me. I've given four friends lists of people to call when I am near death or have died. Nancy's obituary didn't come out until the evening of the services, so nobody would have known if her family and friends hadn't called people. Without my lists, my family and friends wouldn't know who to call.

There are certain people I want with me in my final hours, so I also made a list I call the "Circle List" and gave it to Craig. He put it in his date book so it's handy at all times. I call it the Circle List because I envision these loved ones encircling my bed. I want Craig to stay there until my last breath has been taken and my last heartbeat is over, and probably longer. Whether he wants anyone else there or not is up to him, but I do want him there. I don't want to be left alone.

Buying Time

I don't like the phrase, "We'll make you as comfortable as possible."
In our support group, we talked about what the death sentence
would be, and we agreed that it was having the doctor say,
"We'll make you as comfortable as we can."

In December 1993, when Dr. Spivack was reluctant to tell the Hospice of Marin people that I had only six months to live, I had mixed emotions. One was, "Damn it, I'm ready to go." Another was, "Great, I may have more than six months." Then I thought, "How in the hell am I going to get extra time? Is it going to be really awful?" I guess there's always a chance that the cancer cells could stop growing. It doesn't happen very often. But it could happen. But I was feeling worse and worse, and I kept wishing the wrong thing. I kept wishing I would die.

I said to Dr. Spivack, "Can we figure out what's causing my current pain and fix it? Is this too crazy to ask?"

He said that one kidney was partly blocked, but they didn't want to do anything unless I was feeling pain from it because surgery would spread the cancer cells even more. And that wasn't where the pain was. The pain was in my right side in the front, in the pelvic area, from the tumor that's encroaching on my pelvic organs and compressing them. The largest tumor we knew about was about five centimeters, and it felt big to me. I could feel it in my abdomen, and it hurt.

But then my right kidney filled with fluid, causing a lot of pain. Dr. Spivack suggested three procedures: a nerve block to help numb the pain, a stent to help the kidney drain, and a treatment where they put chemo directly into the liver. He wanted to get started right away, but I balked because I was overwhelmed and wanted to think about it. Also, Matt had a free-throw tournament out of town, and I wanted to go if I could. Dr. Spivack gave me some antibiotics to try to prevent a kidney infection.

The next day I called a doctor in Southern California, Dr. Neil Barth. He's one of the few people trained to do a new treatment the FDA had just approved in which they make a vaccine by mixing healthy cells from your body with Interleukin-2. There are some strong side effects but they only last during the treatment. A friend of my neighbor Diana had had great results with this treatment. Her case was similar to mine; now she had no tumors showing up on her scans and a zero CEA. I had tumors all over the place and a 3,000 CEA. I wanted to know if this treatment was a viable one for me.

Before I called Dr. Barth, I asked my internist, Dr. Oppenheim, "Could I be a candidate for this treatment? If so, what are the possibilities for any kind of quality life afterward? If not, are there any other aggressive treatments out there? Or is it time to stop all treatments and, if so, what's the easiest, fastest, most painless way for me to let go?"

Dr. Oppenheim said, "God, you're a tough broad."

I said, "No, I'm just taking care of myself. I've had to do that since the beginning. You know, I wasn't supposed to live until Christmas of 1992. If I hadn't asked all these questions and been a tough broad, I wouldn't be around today."

He said, "That's for sure. You know, certain people recommended you turn your lights out a couple of months ago."

I said, "That's what I want to know. Is it time?"

Dr. Oppenheim called an oncologist friend at the Mayo Clinic who said that under no circumstances would they recommend the Interleukin-2 vaccine treatment for me. It had only an 11 percent response rate. It's only been shown to be effective on kidney cancer, and they didn't even know that Dr. Barth was doing it with colon cancer. They also said the side effects could be fatal.

Dr. Oppenheim talked to his friend about another new drug, but the friend said because I already had some lung involvement, they would not recommend that treatment either. What his friend said, basically, was that I had failed the systemic chemo route and I should stop treatment, except for palliative treatments to take care of pain. He agreed with Dr. Spivack that they should do the nerve block and the kidney stent, but he didn't think they should do the third procedure, putting chemo right into the liver. Dr. Spivack said, "We'd only consider that if the pain wasn't controlled by the first two." Dr. Spivack also said he would not recommend the Interleukin-2 vaccine.

Dr. Barth's nurse called me back after the doctor looked at my current medical summaries and said he also did not recommend the Interleukin-2 treatment. It was too late, she said. Everybody seemed to agree that I should only do things to help control my pain and keep me comfortable for however long it takes for my body to do itself in. It was disappointing. The Interleukin-2 vaccine was sort of a pie-in-the-sky hope. But when I reviewed my CT scan summary, it reminded me of what I probably already knew. It was pretty clear things had spread beyond the point of no return and that I was in the waiting game.

Was I upset? Yes. Angry? Yes. I still didn't know how much time I had, and I still hadn't gotten an answer to my question, "What's the best and fastest way to go?" All the doctors seemed to be saying was, "We don't know. Your body will take whatever course it's going to take, and you're going to be stuck with whatever it is."

In February 1994 Dr. Spivack called to say, "Your creatinine test results were very bad." That's a test that measures kidney output. I only had one working kidney—tumors had shut the right one down completely. He said, "You've got to have your left kidney stented immediately."

A specialist called a "special interventions radiologist" performs the procedure because it is done utilizing an X-ray and computer so they can see where they're going. They would go into my back with a needle and pull a tube from my back into my kidney, into the ureters, and down into the bladder. The tube is like a long straw. It would allow my kidney to drain into the bladder so I could urinate normally, and if it gets blocked again, I could drain urine out the tube that comes out my back. I would have to have it replaced every six to eight weeks.

My urologist tried to discourage me from doing the procedure. He felt that if I didn't do it, they could "make me comfortable" and that within about ten days I would die of uremic poisoning. But I wasn't ready. It wasn't time yet.

I felt as if the urologist was trying to make me feel guilty for wanting to live longer. He said I made him feel "uncomfortable" with all my questions. I asked him what it would be like to die of uremic poisoning. It seemed to me that if he thought I should decline the procedure, he should feel comfortable talking about what my death would be like.

He said, "Why does it matter to you what it will be like when I have promised we will make you comfortable?"

I said, "Because I have been promised for two years that I'd be made comfortable, and I haven't been comfortable yet."

I kept wondering how he could look at me and see somebody who looked as healthy as I did, and tell me it was time to die. Would he say the same thing to his wife? His child? His mother?

I was passionately afraid, angry, and upset in the hospital. My nurses were upset; my family was upset; everybody was upset. Everyone knew I didn't have much time, and I think some people probably agreed with the urologist.

The doctor who did the procedure was also extremely cold. He gave me a warning at the beginning: "If you complain too much, I will stop the procedure." They didn't give me anesthesia.

They gave me morphine and local painkillers but I felt every poke and pull of that tube deep inside my body. It was extremely painful. At one point, I said, "Can you tell me what you're doing," because I thought if I knew what the play-by-play was, I could understand why it hurt and when it was going to be over.

He said, "If I talk to you, I'm going to lose my concentration." The nurse, who was fantastic, came over and held my hand. I gripped her hands so hard, she must have been in pain too.

They must have given me some kind of amnesiac drug at the end, because the doctor asked me later, "Do you remember anything?"

I said, "Yes, I remember everything."

He was very surprised. He said, "You do?" And I still do. It was miserable.

I felt almost too embarrassed to call him the next week when I knew I had cystitis. He had made me feel ashamed of myself for asking questions. He had accused me of making life difficult for him. I don't think he even understood that his "discomfort" was nothing in comparison to mine. I felt guilty to be alive. Twice so far in my cancer experience I have had to speak up for myself to save my life. The colorectal surgeon who did not want to perform a colostomy to give me more time and the urologist who discouraged me from getting a stent to prevent uremic poisoning held their beliefs so strongly they were willing to "make me comfortable" and let me die rather than discuss my opinions and concerns. Doctors are not gods, nor are patients, but I believe the first objective should be to consider what the patient wants and is willing to do.

My time is short, I think. I hope it doesn't drag out so that I'm miserable for a lot of it. Somebody said they couldn't understand how I could say, "That's it, I've had enough." I said, "Imagine that you've got the worst flu you've ever had in your life, with every inch of your body involved, a stiff neck, a headache, a complete body ache, a high temperature. You feel terrible all over and you don't think you're going to ever come out of it. Your doctor says, 'Guess what, I've got this great medicine for you. This medicine will keep you alive a lot longer. The only hitch is, you will never feel better than you feel right now; in fact, while you're on this medicine you will actually feel worse.'" In other words, I could take another type of chemo, but they've all been shown to be less effective than the chemo I've already taken. And it would make me even sicker. So what's the point?

The Waiting Game

I'm in a holding pattern. Some days I feel really good,
and some days I can't get out of bed. I don't know whether
I'm living or dying. I feel as if I'm in God's waiting room,
waiting for the next organ to fail.

Around the holiday season and into January of 1994, I was feeling pretty good. I did some Christmas shopping. I drove my car. I wasn't on chemo or any other kind of treatment, and the effects of the radiation were finally gone.

When I started feeling better, my attitude about dying changed immediately. I told my doctor, "I was ready to die in November, now here I am, feeling fairly good. Am I well enough to have a treatment to slow things down, or do we stop and let me enjoy the time I have left?" He suggested waiting until the end of January when we would take another CT scan and see how things had progressed.

When I see myself looking well, I want to *be* well. I want to think things have skidded to a halt for a while. I would be delighted if the cancer suddenly went into remission, even though I'd still be in poor health, and there's nothing I can do to feel completely comfortable. Sometimes I have a lot of energy, even enough to go out and do something. The next day I'll lie in bed wondering how I can even get up to go to the doctor. But I could live this way for a long time, because it's not unbearable.

As soon as I felt better, the fear got worse. In November I felt so awful that I welcomed the idea of not waking up in the morning. But in January, every time I got a new pain, I was terrified: "Is this going to be it? Is my kidney failing? Has my liver stopped working?" A pain near my colon would make me think, "I'm getting another blockage." Another blockage would kill me, and very quickly. The idea of going from feeling good to being dead overnight terrifies me.

In February 1994, I wrote this poem in Craig's book.

What It's Like

Doctors making dire predictions
Laboratory tests and scans providing certain evidence
Tumors tearing out space to grow in old and new places
The body shrinking only in overall size from failing interest in
   nourishment
Still the mind refusing to give in, rallying each morning upon
   waking once again

By the end of February I couldn't believe I was still alive. My energy was coming in very short spurts. I couldn't get out of bed very often or go very far, because of pain and lack of energy. I was down to ninety-seven pounds. I couldn't eat much at a time. My stomach didn't empty itself out, so when I tried to put something new in, there was no room, and everything would come up. I kept trying to force myself to eat. One weekend, Craig made a huge stew, beef and carrots and potatoes, and it tasted wonderful. Judy Hubbard made chicken soup, and another friend, Jean Cook, brought over a nice vegetable soup and two loaves of homebaked bread. Foods like that were appealing, and they were easy to eat and keep down. Carol Ware baked some Cornish hens that she had marinated with apricots and sherry. Sue Darling and her husband Brent Ort kept bringing me tantalizing meals. My mom and Craig's mom exhausted themselves shopping for and cooking anything I wanted. Everyone made it impossible for me to decline food, and eventually I began eating again and gained a few pounds.

I had all this overwhelming proof staring me in the face that I was going to die and, according to some of my doctors, very soon. But I hadn't given in to it yet. I still found it extremely difficult to believe, even though the mirror showed a shrinking body that looked like a Holocaust victim, just bones and skin. The skin hung off my body as if it wasn't even connected, funny little folds of skin where there used to be some bulk. It was shocking to see myself undressed—my abdomen and back were a landscape of scars, openings, tubes, bags, bandages, and dressings.

For a while, my To Do list hung over me like an ominous cloud. I wondered, "How much time do I have? How much energy will I have? Where do I want to spend it? What about all these high-priority things? Am I going to get them all done?" I prayed, "Please don't let me die in the middle. I want to do all these things so badly." But I've mellowed out about that. If they get done, they get done, and if they don't, they don't. All that became less and less important as my energy began to wane.

Oren Harari told me a myth about a young man who was going to die and was told by one of the gods that if he could find somebody to take his place, he would be allowed to live longer. He went to his older relatives and asked them to take his disease. He asked one relative who had only two years to live, "Will you trade places with me?"

The relative said, "No, I won't."

"Why not?" the young man asked. "You only have a few years left anyway."

The relative said, "Yes, but I do have two years. They're mine, and I want them."

That's how I feel. I'm not going to fold up my tent when I still have some camping to do.

I don't know what's going to happen next. Whatever it is, I know the doctors won't be able to do anything about it. I could die overnight. My colon could perforate. I could have kidney failure, liver failure, another blockage, a serious infection. In any case, I'll probably go into a coma for a day or two and that will be it. I'm just trying to put it off as long as I can. I'm dreading it, and even after all this time, I'm still finding it hard to believe. It just amazes me. When the time comes, I want to be able to say, "I'm ready," and then have the lights go out. Or the light come on, depending on what happens when death occurs. I thought by the time I got to this stage I would be ready. But I'm not. I'm just not.

The Most Important Journey

&

I'm not concerned about death. I worry more about the dying part. The scary thing is the process of dying, not knowing what that's going to be like, quick or slow, painful or not.

In 1986 I visited my ex-sister-in-law, Susan Robinson, a few weeks before she died. While Susan was sleeping in her bedroom, doing her business of dying, those of us who were visiting, her family members and anybody else who happened to stop by, would congregate in the kitchen and talk. We'd talk about how Susan was doing and when she was due for her next morphine shot; we'd talk about our lives; we'd talk about the weather. I remember feeling uncomfortable about that. Here Susan was, taking the most important journey of her lifetime, and we were in the kitchen eating and talking and carrying on. It was like a death watch. We'd take turns going in and sitting with her, but it was creepy. I don't know if it bothered her—I'm embarrassed to say that I never asked—but I don't want that to happen to me. I don't want to be off in the bedroom dying while everybody else is having a good old time in the kitchen, going on about their lives while I'm trying to grasp the last little bits of mine.

I wonder how I will die, what it's going to be like, and how it will affect those around me. I talked about how I felt to my pastor, Dave Steele. I said, "I don't like the idea of my family having to go through all this. I'm especially worried about Matthew seeing me die."

What he said was very comforting. He said, "It can be a wonderful experience to be with somebody who is letting go of life." He said that a surprise death, where someone dies unexpectedly from a heart attack or an accident, seems to be harder on the families than watching the dying person lose their ability to do things, and to see the peacefulness and the acceptance of death. He said, "It will probably be a wonderful experience for your husband and your child, even though they're going to be enormously sad. During those final days, you will let go of the big crowd and begin to focus in on a core group of people who you want to see and who want to share this experience with you. Also, some people will start moving themselves out as it gets worse because it's so fearful." That was good for me to hear because it helped me see what's in store. It was also comforting to hear that I would find peace and acceptance in time.

Letting Go

Every time I'm offered a treatment, I have to decide whether to accept it or deny it. I constantly have to ask the hard questions. I think family members have to be sensitive to whether the person they love is ready to give up or not. If their loved one is not ready to let go, help in the fight. If the person is ready, support him or her and help pull up the covers.

After the colostomy, the doctors advised me to go back on radiation, to reduce the tumors pressing on my colon, ureters, and other organs.

Craig and I started talking about four o'clock one morning, after I'd gotten up to take some medicine. I wasn't feeling good, and I started to cry. He said, "Are you crying?"

"No!"

"Well, what is this, a tear?"

"Yes."

"Why?"

"Because I'm working so hard to make myself feel better and there's no reward for my work. I'm not feeling well yet, and I wanted to feel great by now. I've had surgery, and now I have to go back onto chemo and radiation and I'm not going to feel good for months. I just hope it's all worth it."

I started asking myself when I was going to say, "That's it, no more." I had bought some extra time with the radiation and the colostomy, but at that time I couldn't think of any moments that had been worth putting up with all the bad ones. It had been boring. I had felt nauseous and miserable.

Craig said, "You know, if halfway through this radiation you decide you've had enough, you can say stop."

I said, "I'm not going to do that. In for a penny, in for a pound."

I knew two people with cancer who decided that they had had enough. One was my neighbor Miriam's brother, who had liver cancer. He had been an alcoholic and had a bad liver to start with. His doctors gave him only two or three months. He was in a lot of pain, and he was extremely depressed. Miriam tried to get him to see other doctors, to try chemotherapy, but he just said, "No." When she asked how he was doing, he said, "None of your business." She was hurt at first, but she came to see that it was his way of guarding his privacy, of letting go with dignity. He died, as predicted, within a very short time.

A woman in my cancer support group, Joan, stopped coming to meetings. Her doctors had given her very little time. She'd had breast cancer for twelve years, and it metastasized in her abdomen. She could feel the tumors in her abdomen. She had a chemo treatment because her doctor advised her to, and she lost all her hair just months before she died. She was angry. She felt her doctors had misled her—if she had so little time, why did she have to go through all that?

In our support group, when one of us starts talking about giving up, the others tend to say, "Talk to another doctor." "Have you thought about this, have you thought about that?" Even though none of us likes to get advice, we're the first ones to give it. We disguise it with all kinds of communication methods, but we know what we're saying. Joan knew we didn't want her to give up, and she resented our advice. When she stopped coming to group, we realized she was serious, and we learned that there *is* a point when all of us say, "Enough."

Another person in our group talked seriously about suicide. Sometimes I think it's a good idea; cancer is so mean. But then I reflect on when the colorectal surgeon said I had two weeks to live, and I remember how hard I was willing to fight for more time. I think suicide should be an option for people who don't want to fight anymore and are ready to die. They should have the right to say to their doctor, "Okay, that's it, give me a lethal injection." I think Dr. Jack Kevorkian is a pioneer. When you read the cases he's taken on, you can't help but empathize with those people, who clearly made the right decisions for themselves. As more people begin doing it openly, it won't carry such a stigma. There won't be so many people going to therapy because a family member chose suicide. I could consider it an option if Matt were older and could understand why I chose to do it. Why should a kid watch a parent undergo terrible pain and immense indignity in order to have a "normal" death, and then have to listen to well-meaning adults say, "What a blessing that she finally went!"

At Commonweal, we talked about whether we wanted to continue treatment. Some people felt strongly that they would continue fighting until the last breath and others felt they wouldn't. I was very insistent that I wanted to keep fighting. But at that time I still thought there would be a period when I would feel better. And it hasn't come. I'm puzzled and confused and tired of struggling day after day, of trying to decide whether to call the doctor, of delicately balancing the pain and the pills, of dragging myself to doctors' offices to get something new "looked at," of having to take naps because I can't control my flagging energy, of making and breaking dates with friends, of forcing myself to eat, and on, and on.

It's sad because I know a lot of people are out there rooting for me. I feel like everybody wants me to fight. It's strange, but I've never felt that I was fighting. People say that word a lot,

"I'm fighting for my life." My friends who also have cancer use it. They say, "It's a big fight, it's a battle." But I don't. I'm just trying to keep up with it. It's more like coping. If I have a big roaring pain right now, and I think, "Well, that's the biggest pain I've ever had in my life," I can still say to myself, "Can you handle pain like that? Yes, I can. I just handled it. I'm on the other side of it. I can have another pain like that and still come out on the other side and watch a TV program with my kid or go feed the fish with my family or have a nice dinner." Everything that becomes a known becomes tolerable.

Everybody says I've been courageous up to this point, so why not keep going. But the mind and body are wearing out. I don't know how much longer I want to keep going. It's hard to tell people that. They can understand if they see me in severe pain, or looking pale, drawn or obviously ill. But I'm not always in severe pain, and I usually look well. People still say, "You look so good!" as if that were a barometer for longevity. They don't see what it takes for me to get out of bed, get dressed, and get through the day.

The question is, why do I keep wanting to wake up every day when I have all this pain and annoyance? I guess it comes down to the fact that I've gotten used to living this way. My fear is of what I don't know, of what's going to happen next. That's totally out of my control.

What's important now is waking up. Finding a few moments each day where I feel good enough to say that I enjoyed myself. It's like keeping things in balance. There's got to be some place where the balance shifts and I'm going to say, "It's not worth waking up any more to face this." Even with all the pain, and all the major and minor annoyances with things that work and don't work in my body, the scale is still in favor of waking up. But one of these days it won't be.

I don't know what I'm going to do the next time a doctor says, "Here are your options." I don't know what my decision's going to be. I'm tired. I'm tired of suffering and of watching other people watch me suffer. I don't know how much more of it I'm willing to do. I don't know how many more times I'm going to let doctors touch me. It's painful and undignified. I'm bored with living with cancer. I desperately want to live, but not just as a spectator.

Linda Pratt Mukai

Linda Pratt Mukai died in San Anselmo, CA Oct. 11, 1994 surrounded by family and friends. Loving wife of Craig D. Mukai, DDS. Loving mother of Matthew, age 9. Dearest daughter of Dorothy M. Anderhub of Norman, OK and James Pratt, Jr. of Tucson, AZ. Beloved sister of Susan Pratt of Scottsdale, AZ.

A native of Norman, OK, aged 48 years. A graduate of University of Oklahoma at Norman class of 1968. Owner of Linda Mukai and Associates in San Anselmo, CA. A former marketing and human resources manager for Shaklee Corp., Amfac, Inc. and Federated Department Stores and a consultant to the San Francisco Chamber of Commerce.

Friends are invited to attend the Funeral Sat., Oct. 15, 1994 at 10 a.m. at Christ Presbyterian Church, 620 Del Ganado Rd., Terra Linda, San Rafael, CA. Interment Valley Memorial Park Cemetery, Novato, CA. Friends may call for visitation at the mortuary from 9 a.m. - 9 p.m. Fri. Memorial contributions preferred to Marin General Hospital Foundation, Shared Care Unit, P.O. Box 8010, San Rafael, CA 94912, Christ Presbyterian Church or Hospice of Marin, 150 Nellen Dr., Corte Madera, CA 94925

Keaton's Mortuary
1022 E St.
San Rafael, CA
415-453-0571

Craig

Almost as soon as Linda was gone, I felt as if I'd fallen into a huge void. I didn't have anything to grasp onto. My family and friends were there, but they were not really anchors. They were all swimming, too, out of kilter. Everyone was reaching for something.

I've never contemplated suicide. But the moment Linda died I had this overwhelming urge to go where she went. The feeling was so dramatic. I thought, "I've done a lot in my lifetime, I've completed everything, and I want to go with her. Wherever she went, I want to go along." I don't know how long it lasted. It seemed like a long time, but it probably wasn't more than fifteen or twenty seconds.

I can't remember who I was talking with, but the person said, "It's like you're standing in the middle of the road and you see a Mack truck coming at you at about sixty miles an hour. How can you really imagine how bad it's going to hurt when that truck hits you?"

I think you need to be counseled about what it means to lose someone you love, to be taught before the final climax of the life scenario, before everything starts to fall apart. Then you can recover faster, because you'll have a safety net waiting when you fall. I didn't do that. I would have liked to have had someone say, "I know you may feel you don't need counseling right now, but why don't we just sit down and talk for a short period of time?"

Even if I'd said, "I don't think I really need it," it would have helped for someone to say, "Listen, we've found that it's necessary. You are going to have to go through a serious grieving process; maybe we can help you through, point out some of the pitfalls you're going to encounter. You think you know where you're going, but you really don't. You don't understand the depths to which despair and grief and anger and all those things start to change you."

That was the one aspect I'd forgotten. My needs. My need to have a wife and a complete family and have the one I love the most be there for me, for my son, for everybody. It was something I hadn't really thought about and hadn't planned for. I wasn't shown by anybody how to grieve, and then how to rise up out of the ashes. Everyone goes through this at some point, mothers, fathers, uncles and aunts, sisters and brothers, wives and husbands, but until you do, you don't have a clue about what's going on. Hospice and Commonweal can really help.

I think the thing that finally got me through is feeling that I didn't lose her. I don't say, "As long as she's in my memory she's alive." I say, "She's in my memory, but she's not still alive. She's incorporated into my soul. She's in my conscious thought." When I mess up with Matt, maybe yell too much, I can hear her saying, "Come on, Craig, relax, back off." I can see her in my actions, in my thought patterns. I will never lose her because she is literally a part of me. I can hear her talking to me. I can imagine what she would say about what I did or am about to do. It's more than just remembering who she was; it's learning from her and honoring her when I know that she knew a little bit more about something than I did. Once I realized that she wasn't just a memory but a living part of everything I do, that she can still help guide me and help me raise our son, it was easier to say, "Okay, I can let her body and her spirit go, but I won't let go of that portion of her soul that's still mine."

The way Linda handled death and dying has and always will have a profound effect on me. I've seen how to live and die with grace, so I no longer fear death. I hope that I will handle the dying process with as much grace and dignity as she did.

Everyone has to die, and everyone has to watch people die. Everyone goes through the grieving process. I can imagine that some people never come out of it, but if you don't come out of it you've let the loved one down. It takes a while. You have to have a reason to live, as I have in my son. If you can find that reason, it helps bring you back.

Epilogue

I wasn't in the circle of friends and family around Linda's bed when she died. I was several hundred miles away, in a hotel room in San Pedro, California. I was doing what Linda should have been doing, preparing for a training session while watching sailboats bob in the harbor beneath my window and, beyond, the ocean stretching blue to the horizon.

After my husband called to tell me that Linda had died the night before, I set my work aside and sat at the window for a long time, weeping with sadness and relief. Sadness at losing someone who had become a dear, dear friend. Relief that her long and difficult journey had finally come to an end.

I'd already said goodbye. When I visited with Linda two nights earlier, she was drifting in and out of consciousness, trying to talk but unable to communicate. Her words, when she could form them, were garbled and almost impossible to understand. She recognized me, though, and seemed to have things she still wanted to say. I held her hand and told her not to talk—telling Linda not to talk!—because it took so much effort and was so frustrating for her. I talked instead, telling her not to worry about the book, that it would be finished, somehow. That her story would be told. I said I loved her, and with great effort she managed the words, "I love you, Janis."

When the sun finally sank into the ocean, I dried my eyes and went back to work. To my surprise, I hardly cried during the next few days. I thought that perhaps I'd already done my grieving. After all, Linda and I had wept together from the beginning, whenever we got too close to the pain. I had cried again and again when explaining Linda's condition to my friends and family, and I'd often found myself in tears when working on the book, especially on the parts relating to Matt and Craig and Linda's mother.

Still, the tears began again in earnest when I entered the crowded church the following Saturday for Linda's memorial service, and they continued throughout the ride to the cemetary where we all gathered around her coffin to say our last goodbyes. Dave Steele was right. The people who survive you need a service. They need to gather together, so they can grieve together. They need a chance to say goodbye.

Linda was forty-eight years old when she died at 8:20 p.m. on Tuesday, October 11, 1994. It had been two years and four months, almost to the day, since she learned she was terminally ill.

As Linda had planned, she died at home. Craig was there, of course, and Matt. The two "Moms," Dottie and March. Her friends Sue, Brent, and Diana were also with her, as they had been throughout her long journey.

As Linda had hoped, she died peacefully and without pain. After she had taken her last breath, Craig disconnected the machines and removed the tubes from her body. Everyone cried and said their goodbyes late into the night. Craig did not permit Linda's body to be moved until the next morning.

The week after Linda's death was filled with the rituals we use to honor the deceased among us and to begin the grieving process. On Wednesday morning her friends activated the telephone tree she had set up so people could be informed of her passing. There was a one-day period for viewing her body at a funeral home, a tradition from her Oklahoma childhood. Craig wrote a loving obituary that appeared in two local newspapers as well as in newspapers in Norman, Oklahoma, and Tacoma, Washington, Linda and Craig's home towns.

The funeral service was held on Saturday, October 15, at Linda's church, Christ Presbyterian in Terra Linda. The church was filled to overflowing with more than 300 family members, friends, neighbors, acquaintances, and business colleagues who had come to pay tribute and say goodbye.

Linda being Linda, she had designed most of her own service, selecting the speakers and some of the music. The service was beautiful and traditional: hymns, prayers, scripture readings, speakers, a blessing. I was not the only one there who felt strongly that Linda was watching and would have approved.

For her body's final resting place, Linda chose Valley Memorial Park in Novato, a short drive from her San Anselmo home and surrounded by the same green-brown Marin County hills. After a brief graveside service, Craig and Matt invited us all back to the house. It was a sunny fall day. We wandered in and out of the house and talked in small groups in the newly landscaped back yard, one of Linda's final projects. The memorial gathering was catered by Comforts, the San Anselmo restaurant that had catered Linda and Craig's Celebration of Life party only sixteen months earlier.

Several months after Linda's death, when the trees outside my office window were lush and green and the flowers on the deck below were in full bloom, I began, finally, to think about the ending to this book. To try making sense of Linda's journey, to consider what it meant to me and others who had known her. As I reviewed the still-unfinished manuscript, I saw that when we began our work, I'd never experienced the death of anyone close to me. That had changed. During the two-and-a-half year span of Linda's illness, I lost two uncles and an aunt. My friend Jay had died of cancer. Duncan Craven, my children's peer who I had known since he was three days old, had fallen through thin ice in Denmark while skating in the early morning hours with his girlfriend. And then my father, who, like Linda, loved life and stubbornly refused to give it up even though severe heart disease had kept him in and out of the hospital since February, passed away in the early hours on May 6, 1995, almost three years after Linda was diagnosed with cancer.

In the Prologue, I wrote that when Linda asked me to help her with this book, she was giving me a gift. And she has, a very precious gift: a new wisdom. I've learned so much. For one thing, I've learned that death is final. One moment a person you love is alive. Then he or she is gone, and that is that. There is nothing you can do. All the wanting in the world won't bring the person back.

Now I understand why we revere life above all, and why the life we love is the most precious thing there is, more precious even than our own. And as I grieve for the loss of those I love, I am struck by the fragility of life, by how little we are able to control our destiny, and by how rapidly our lives can change. I have always counted on having a future, and I believed that my future was mine to shape. I know now, not intellectually, not in an abstract way, but *know*, that certainty is an illusion. I can hope, and I can dream. But my dreams are not reality. The reality is that I cannot control the future, nor can I be sure that it will even come. The only thing I can be sure of is *now*.

Linda's death is a yellow flag, a caution. A reminder to live my life as it happens, instead of speeding through, or floating by. Those days when I'm running too fast to smell the roses, I sometimes feel that she is standing nearby with her hand upraised as if to say, "Hold on a minute. Take a good look around. *Be here now.*" I remember my flirtation with Zen Buddhism in the late 1960s, when I learned that focussing on my breathing would bring myself back to the now from whatever future or past I kept trying to capture or recapture. Linda learned that lesson. She learned to slow down and live each moment to the fullest. She jettisoned the unimportant, re-ordered her priorities, and learned how to live her life, because she realized that it was the only life she was going to have.

The year following Linda's death has been a time for grieving and for healing, a time for her family to put their lives back together. After the funeral, Dottie stayed with Craig and Matt for several weeks, then returned to Norman, Oklahoma where she has her own circle of friends. She returned to San Anselmo for Christmas, and she comes back from time to time for brief visits. Jim Pratt, Linda's father, who was already very ill by the time Linda died, was able to attend the memorial service but died of his colon cancer only eight months later, on June 26, 1995. (Only eleven days after Linda's death, Linda and Craig's friend Chris Jang also died.) Craig's parents return often to visit and help with Matt.

As Linda had hoped, Craig has stayed in the home they built together. He is working hard to build a new life for himself and Matt, organizing his work schedule so he can spend as much time with his son as possible. Matt is now in the fifth grade and doing well. "He's more clingy," Craig says, "which would be expected. I always have to let him know I'm going to be here. But he's a tough kid. I don't think he can verbalize a lot of this. But he's been spectacular.

"In their religion class in school," he adds, "they were talking about the different terms they use for God. Matt wrote, 'Mom Protector.' For him, I think that's exactly what's going on. I'm really proud of him. He's my star basketball player, my number one draft pick in baseball. A super guy."

Linda has been gone for almost a year. I think about her at least once a day, and I miss her. I miss our talks, which became deeper and richer and more intimate as her illness progressed. I miss her quick wit. I miss her perception, being able to ask, "How would you approach this one?" and knowing I would get a careful hearing and good ideas. I miss the tennis games we never played and the walks we were too busy to take.

But I agree with Craig: Linda lives on, in a way, as does my father, as part of me. I am different because they touched me. Affected me. Changed me. I see now that when someone dies we grieve for the loss of that individual consciousness, that personality, that physical being we can see and touch and talk with. Perhaps we forget to notice how much of the person we still have.

And from Linda, I also have the life lessons I learned:

Value my friendships. Remember that people are more important than tasks. Make time for my friends, and be open to developing new friendships. Linda made some of her best friends during the final months of her life.

Appreciate what people have to give, and do not expect what they are unable to give. Friendships are based on different things. Some people are at their best when everything is going well, some when there's a crisis. Recognize what my relationships are based on, and value that, instead of expecting people to be different than they are.

Expect change. Nothing stays the same. Change gives me a chance to learn and grow, even when the changes are not ones I'd choose.

Live the moments of my life. Learn from the past. Anticipate the future. But keep in mind that the only time I'm actually alive is *now*, and *now*, and *now*. To help me remember, focus on my breathing.

Make things happen for myself, and remember that the journey is as important as the destination. Maybe I won't get there; so what? The journey creates the experiences, and it's the experiences that I live.

Accept what I cannot change. I could waste a perfectly good life waiting for that lucky break, trying to force other people to be different, wishing I was taller or thinner or younger or more beautiful. Go for what I can change, and what's worth changing, and forget about things I can't control.

Acknowledge my successes. One of Linda's great pleasures during her illness was the recognition that she had succeeded in her business. That she and Craig had created the kind of life they both wanted, and they had done it themselves.

Give something back. Whether it's giving a dollar to a homeless person or teaching someone to read or comforting a sick friend, it feels good to help someone else. I get too busy; I forget; I don't want to get involved. I miss a lot.

Don't blame other people, or myself. I can't fix problems by laying blame. Linda struggled with anger at herself and her doctors for not noticing she was ill until it was too late. She worked hard at letting go of the need to find someone to blame, because she understood that blaming got in her way and distracted her from more important things.

Death is the end of this life, and I believe that this life is all we have. Still, I find it mysterious and magical that this collection of atoms, this certain formation of matter, should know itself, and I think that something of that unique consciousness does remain.

More than anything, Linda was a person who knew herself, and she continued to learn and grow, right until the end. She believed she could improve both people and events, and she did. Never one to do anything by halves, she worked as hard at the business of staying alive and at finding more satisfying ways to connect with others as she had at building her consulting business. She worked hard to find ways of extending her life beyond its span, of leaving something of herself in other people, of contributing something of value from her experience with dying. As one of those she left behind, I am a better person for having known her.

Goodbye, Linda. And thanks for the lovely gift.

Janis Chan
San Anselmo, California
September 1995

Linda, Craig, and Matt Mukai
March 1992

RESOURCES

Support Services

American Cancer Society   404-320-3333
1599 Clifton Road N.E.
Atlanta, GA 30329

The Cancer Information Service   1-800-4-CANCER
National Cancer Institute (a division of federal   (1-800-4-6237)
National Institute for Health) hot line

Cancer Support and Education Center   415/327-6166
1035 Pine, Menlo Park, CA

Center for Attitudinal Healing   415/331-6161
Sausalito, CA

Commonweal   415/868-0970
Bolinas, CA

Medical Information Service   1-800/999-1999
On-line computer search service

National Hospice Organization   703/243-5900
1901 North Moore Street, Suite 901
Arlington, VA 22209

National Library of Medicine   301/402-5874
Cancer FAX information available by fax
Medline computer literature search, available
in medical/ health libraries and hospitals

Susan G. Komen Breast Cancer Foundation   1-800-I'M AWARE
5005 LBJ Freeway, Suite 370   (1-800-462-9273)
Dallas, TX 75244

Books on Cancer

∽

The Alpha Institute. *The Alpha Book on Cancer and Living: for Patients, Family and Friends.* 1993. The Alpha Institute, P.O. Box 2463, Alameda, CA, 800/866-4111.

Anderson, Greg. *50 Essential Things to Do When the Doctor Says it's Cancer.* 1993. Plume, New York.

Block, Annette. *Fighting Cancer.* 1985. Pocket Books.

Dollinger, Malin, Ernest H. Rosenbaum with Greg Cable. *Everyone's Guide to Cancer Therapy.* 1991. Andrews and McMeel, Kansas City, MO.

Harpham, Wendy Schlessel. *After Cancer: A Guide to Your New Life.* 1994. W.W. Norton, New York.

Holleb, Arthur, ed. *American Cancer Society Cancer Book.* 1986. Doubleday, Garden City, NJ.

Kauffman, Danette G. *Surviving Cancer.* 1987. Acropolis Books.

LeShan, Lawrence. *Cancer as a Turning Point.* 1989. Dutton, New York.

Lang, Susan S. and Richard B. Patt. *You Don't Have to Suffer.* 1994. Oxford University Press, New York.

Love, Susan M., with Karen Lindsey. *Dr. Susan Love's Breast Book,* 2nd edition. 1995. Addison-Wesley, Reading, MA.

McAllister, Robert M., Sylvia Teich Horowitz and Raymond V. Gilden. *Cancer: What Cutting-Edge Science Can Tell You and Your Doctor About the Causes of Cancer and the Impact on Diagnosis and Treatment.* 1993. Basic Books, New York.

McKay, Judith and Nancee Hirano. *The Chemotherapy Survival Guide.* 1993. New Harbinger Publications, 5674 Shattuck Ave., Oakland, CA.

Morra, Marion and Eve Potts. *Choices.* 1980. Avon, New York.

Pelton, Ross and Lee Overholser. *Alternatives in Cancer Therapy.* 1994. Simon & Schuster, New York.

Rollin, Betty. *First, You Cry.* 1976. Lippincott, Philadelphia, PA.

Rosenberg, Steven A. and John M. Barry. *The Transformed Cell: Unlocking the Mysteries of Cancer.* 1992. Putnam, New York.

Books on Healing

Carter, Rosalynn. *Helping Yourself Help Others.* 1994. Times Books, New York.

Chopra, Deepak. *Creating Health: Beyond Prevention, Toward Perfection.* 1987. Houghton Mifflin, Boston.

Chopra, Deepak. *Quantum Healing.* 1989. Bantam Books, New York.

Cousins, Norman. *Anatomy of an Illness.* 1979. W.W. Norton, New York.

Cousins, Norman. *Head First: The Biology of Hope.* 1989. Dutton, New York.

Dossey, Larry. *Healing Words.* 1993. HarperSan Francisco, San Francisco.

Eisenberg, David with Thomas Lee Wright. *Encounters with Qi: Exploring Chinese Medicine.* 1985. W.W. Norton, New York.

Foundation for Inner Peace. *A Course in Miracles* (text, workbook, and teacher's manual). 1975. Foundation for Inner Peace. Tiburon, CA.

Hausman, Patricia and Judith Benn Hurley. *The Healing Foods.* 1989. Rodale Press, Emmaus, PA.

Jampolsky, Gerald. *Teach Only Love: The Seven Principles of Attitudinal Healing.* 1983. Bantam Books, New York.

Kabat-Zinn, Jon. *Full Catastrophe Living.* 1990. Delta, New York.

Kushner, Harold S. *When Bad Things Happen to Good People.* 1981. Schocken Books, New York.

Lerner, Michael, *Choices in Healing.* 1994. MIT Press, Cambridge, MA.

McWilliams, Peter. *You Can't Afford the Luxury of a Negative Thought.* 1988. Prelude Press, Los Angeles.

Metcalf, C.W. and Roma Felible. *Lighten Up: Survival Skills for People Under Pressure.* 1993. Addison-Wesley, Reading, MA.

Moyers, Bill. *Healing and the Mind.* 1993. Doubleday, New York.

Mullam, Fitzhugh and Barbara Hoffman, ed. *Charting the Journey: An Almanac of Practical Resources for Cancer Survivors.* 1990. Consumers Union, Mt. Vernon, NY.

Peale, Norman Vincent. *The Power of Positive Thinking.* 1952. Prentice-Hall, New York.

Pelletier, Kenneth R. *Sound Mind, Sound Body.* 1994. Simon & Schuster, New York.

Siegal, Bernie S. *How to Live Between Office Visits.* 1993. HarperCollins, New York.

Siegal, Bernie S. *Love, Medicine and Miracles.* 1986. Harper Perennial, New York.

Spiegal, David. *Living Beyond Limits.* 1993. Times Books, New York.

Topf, Linda Noble and Hal Zina Bennett. *You Are Not Your Illness.* 1995. Fireside, New York.

Weil, Andrew. *Health and Healing: Understanding Conventional and Alternative Medicine.* 1983. Houghton Mifflin, Boston.

Books on Dying

c:\temp\flourish.png

Anderson, Patricia *Affairs in Order.* 1991. Collier Books, New York.

Beresford, Larry. *The Hospice Handbook.* 1993. Little, Brown, Boston.

Callanan, Maggie and Patricia Kelley. *Final Gifts.* 1992. Poseidon Press, New York.

Grosz, Anton. *Letters to a Dying Friend: What Comes Next.* 1989. Theosophical Publishing House, Wheaton, IL.

Kübler-Ross, Elisabeth. *On Death and Dying.* 1969. Macmillan, New York.

Levine, Stephen. *Meetings at the Edge: Dialogues with the Grieving and the Dying, the Healing and the Healed.* 1984. Anchor Press, Garden City, NJ.

Nuland, Sherwin. *How We Die.* 1993. A.A. Knopf, New York.

Ronpoche, Sogyal. *The Tibetan Book of Living and Dying.* 1992. HarperSan Francisco.

Sankar, Andrea. *Dying at Home: A Family Guide for Caregiving.* 1991. Bantam, New York.

214

Web Sites

Oncolink
http://www.oncolink.upenn.edu/

American Cancer Society, California Division
http://www.ca.cancer.org/

MedWeb (links to biomedical Internet resources)
http://www.cc.emory.edu/WHSCL/medweb.html